Photograph on page 1 copyright © Shutterstock.com.

Pictured on the front cover: Super Chocolate Cookies *(page 7)*.

Pictured on the back cover: Pistachio Lemon Shortbread Cookies *(page 28)*, Double Chocolate Dream Bars *(page 96)*, Oat, Chocolate and Hazelnut Biscotti *(page 176)*, Chocolate Hazelnut Sandwich Cookies *(page 125)*, Lemon Squares *(page 149)*, Chocolate Pretzel Cookies *(page 75)*, Classic Chocolate Chip Cookies *(page 32)* and Black and White Cookies *(page 38)*.

ISBN: 978-1-64030-865-7

Manufactured in China.

8 7 6 5 4 3 2 1

Microwave Cooking: Microwave ovens vary in wattage. Use the cooking times as guidelines and check for doneness before adding more time.

WARNING: Food preparation, baking and cooking involve inherent dangers: misuse of electric products, sharp electric tools, boiling water, hot stoves, allergic reactions, foodborne illnesses and the like, pose numerous potential risks. Publications International, Ltd. (PIL) assumes no responsibility or liability for any damages you may experience as a result of following recipes, instructions, tips or advice in this publication.

While we hope this publication helps you find new ways to eat delicious foods, you may not always achieve the results desired due to variations in ingredients, cooking temperatures, typos, errors, omissions, or individual cooking abilities.

Let's get social!

 @Publications_International

 @PublicationsInternational

www.pilcookbooks.com

THE BEST COOKIES

Publications International, Ltd.

CONTENTS

CHIPPERS

GIANT COOKIES

SUGAR & SPICE

CHOCOLATEY BITES

BROWNIES & BARS

SANDWICH COOKIES

FRUIT FLAVORS

SHAPED & ROLLED COOKIES

ETC.

CHIPPERS

SUPER CHOCOLATE COOKIES

Makes about 20 (4-inch) cookies

- 2 cups all-purpose flour
- ⅓ cup unsweetened cocoa powder
- 1 teaspoon baking soda
- ½ teaspoon salt
- 1⅓ cups packed brown sugar
- 1 cup (2 sticks) unsalted butter, softened
- 2 eggs
- 2 teaspoons vanilla
- 1 cup candy-coated chocolate pieces
- 1 cup dried cranberries, dried cherries and/or raisins
- ¾ cup salted peanuts

1. Preheat oven to 350°F. Whisk flour, cocoa, baking soda and salt in medium bowl.

2. Beat brown sugar and butter in large bowl with electric mixer at medium speed 3 to 4 minutes or until light and fluffy. Add eggs and vanilla; beat until well blended. Gradually beat in flour mixture at low speed just until blended. Stir in chocolate pieces, cranberries and peanuts.

3. Drop dough by ¼ cupfuls 3 inches apart onto ungreased cookie sheets. Flatten slightly with fingertips.

4. Bake 13 to 15 minutes or until almost set. Cool on cookie sheets 2 minutes. Remove to wire racks; cool completely.

MOCHA JAVA COOKIES

Makes about 2½ dozen cookies

½ cup (1 stick) unsalted butter, softened

½ cup granulated sugar

½ cup packed brown sugar

1 egg

1½ cups all-purpose flour

2 tablespoons instant espresso powder

1 teaspoon baking soda

½ teaspoon salt

¾ cup semisweet chocolate chips

¾ cup milk chocolate chips

½ cup milk chocolate toffee bits

1. Beat butter, sugars and egg in large bowl with electric mixer at medium speed until blended. Add flour, espresso powder, baking soda and salt; beat at low speed just until combined. Stir in chocolate chips and toffee bits (dough will be stiff). Cover and refrigerate dough 1 hour.

2. Preheat oven to 350°F. Line cookie sheets with parchment paper. Shape dough into 2-inch balls. Place 2 inches apart on prepared cookie sheets. Flatten slightly with fingertips.

3. Bake 7 to 9 minutes or until edges are golden brown. Cool on cookie sheets 5 minutes. Remove to wire racks; cool completely.

CHOCO-ORANGE MACADAMIA COOKIES

Makes about 3 dozen cookies

1 cup macadamia nuts

2 cups plus 1 tablespoon all-purpose flour

½ teaspoon baking powder

½ teaspoon salt

¾ cup (1½ sticks) unsalted butter, melted and cooled

1 cup packed brown sugar

6 tablespoons granulated sugar

2 teaspoons grated orange peel

2 teaspoons vanilla

1 egg

1 egg yolk

1 cup semisweet chocolate chips

½ cup flaked coconut

1. Preheat oven to 350°F.

2. Place macadamias in shallow baking pan. Bake 8 to 10 minutes or until golden brown and fragrant, stirring occasionally. (Nuts burn easily so watch carefully.) Cool completely. Coarsely chop nuts.

3. Whisk flour, baking powder and salt in medium bowl. Beat butter, sugars, orange peel and vanilla in large bowl with electric mixer at medium speed until creamy. Beat in egg and egg yolk until fluffy. Gradually beat in flour mixture at low speed just until blended. Stir in nuts, chocolate chips and coconut.

4. Drop dough by rounded tablespoonfuls 2 inches apart onto ungreased cookie sheets.

5. Bake 10 to 12 minutes or until edges are lightly browned and centers are almost set. Cool on cookie sheets 1 minute. Remove to wire racks; cool completely.

DEEP DARK CHOCOLATE DROPS

Makes about 3 dozen cookies

1¼ cups all-purpose flour

¼ cup unsweetened cocoa powder

½ teaspoon baking soda

½ teaspoon salt

1½ cups semisweet chocolate chips, divided

½ cup (1 stick) unsalted butter, softened

½ cup granulated sugar

¼ cup packed brown sugar

1 egg

2 tablespoons milk

1 teaspoon vanilla

1. Preheat oven to 350°F. Line cookie sheets with parchment paper or lightly grease. Whisk flour, cocoa, baking soda and salt in medium bowl.

2. Place ½ cup chocolate chips in small microwavable bowl. Microwave on HIGH 1 minute; stir. Microwave at additional 30-second intervals until chips are melted and smooth. Let cool slightly.

3. Beat butter and sugars in large bowl with electric mixer at medium speed 3 to 4 minutes or until light and fluffy. Add egg, milk, vanilla and melted chocolate; beat until well blended. Gradually beat in flour mixture at low speed just until blended. Stir in remaining 1 cup chocolate chips. Drop dough 2 inches apart onto prepared cookie sheets.

4. Bake 10 to 11 minutes or until set and no longer shiny. Cool on cookie sheets 2 minutes. Remove to wire racks; cool completely.

OATMEAL S'MORES COOKIES

Makes about 3 dozen cookies

⅔ cup mini marshmallows

2 cups old-fashioned oats

1⅓ cups all-purpose flour

¾ teaspoon baking soda

½ teaspoon baking powder

½ teaspoon salt

1 cup packed brown sugar

¾ cup (1½ sticks) unsalted butter, softened

¼ cup granulated sugar

1 egg

1 tablespoon honey

1 teaspoon vanilla

1 cup semisweet chocolate chips

¾ cup coarse chocolate or honey graham cracker crumbs

1. Cut marshmallows in half. Spread on baking sheet; freeze 1 hour.

2. Preheat oven to 350°F. Line cookie sheets with parchment paper. Combine oats, flour, baking soda, baking powder and salt in medium bowl.

3. Beat brown sugar, butter and granulated sugar in large bowl with electric mixer at medium speed 3 to 4 minutes or until light and fluffy. Add egg, honey and vanilla; beat until well blended. Gradually beat in flour mixture at low speed just until blended. Stir in frozen marshmallows and chocolate chips.

4. Drop dough by rounded tablespoonfuls onto prepared cookie sheets; sprinkle evenly with graham cracker crumbs.

5. Bake about 12 minutes or until puffed and golden. Cool on cookie sheets 5 minutes. Remove to wire racks; cool completely.

OATMEAL-CHIP CRISPIES

Makes about 6 dozen cookies

2 cups all-purpose flour

2 cups old-fashioned oats

1 teaspoon baking powder

1 teaspoon baking soda

½ teaspoon salt

1 cup (2 sticks) unsalted butter, softened

1 cup packed brown sugar

¾ cup granulated sugar

2 eggs

2 tablespoons orange juice

1 teaspoon grated orange peel

1 cup dried cranberries

⅔ cup white chocolate chips

⅔ cup semisweet chocolate chips

1. Preheat oven to 350°F. Line cookie sheets with parchment paper. Combine flour, oats, baking powder, baking soda and salt in medium bowl.

2. Beat butter and sugars in large bowl with electric mixer at medium speed 3 to 4 minutes or until light and fluffy. Add eggs, orange juice and peel; beat 1 minute. Gradually beat in flour mixture at low speed just until blended. Stir in cranberries and chocolate chips.

3. Shape dough into 1-inch balls; place 2 inches apart on prepared cookie sheets. Flatten slightly.

4. Bake 12 to 15 minutes or until lightly browned and firm to the touch. Cool cookies on cookie sheets 2 minutes. Remove to wire racks; cool completely.

DARK CHOCOLATE
⋛ WHITE CHOCOLATE COOKIES ⋛

Makes 3 dozen cookies

4 ounces unsweetened chocolate

2 cups all-purpose flour

1½ teaspoons baking powder

¾ teaspoon salt

1½ cups packed brown sugar

¾ cup (1½ sticks) butter, softened

1 teaspoon vanilla

2 eggs

1 package (12 ounces) white chocolate chips

1. Preheat oven to 350°F. Melt unsweetened chocolate according to package directions; cool slightly.

2. Whisk flour, baking powder and salt in medium bowl. Beat brown sugar, butter and vanilla in large bowl with electric mixer at medium speed 3 to 4 minutes or until light and fluffy. Add eggs; beat until well blended. Beat in melted chocolate. Gradually beat in flour mixture at low speed just until blended. Stir in white chocolate chips.

3. Drop by heaping tablespoonfuls 2 inches apart onto ungreased cookie sheets.

4. Bake 10 minutes or just until set. Cool on cookie sheets 1 minute. Remove to wire racks; cool completely.

WHITE CHOCOLATE MACADAMIA COOKIES

Makes about 3 dozen cookies

1¾ cups all-purpose flour

½ teaspoon salt

¼ teaspoon baking soda

1½ cups packed brown sugar

⅔ cup shortening

1 tablespoon water

1 teaspoon vanilla

2 eggs

1 cup white chocolate chips

1 cup macadamia nuts,
   coarsely chopped

1. Preheat oven to 375°F. Whisk flour, salt and baking soda in medium bowl.

2. Beat brown sugar, shortening, water and vanilla in large bowl with electric mixer at medium speed until well blended. Add eggs; beat 1 minute. Gradually beat in flour mixture at low speed just until blended. Stir in white chocolate chips and nuts.

3. Drop dough by rounded tablespoonfuls 2 inches apart onto ungreased cookie sheets.

4. Bake 7 to 9 minutes or just until set. *Do not overbake.* Cool on cookie sheets 2 minutes. Remove to wire racks; cool completely.

PEANUTTY DOUBLE CHIP COOKIES

Makes about 3 dozen cookies

½ **cup (1 stick) unsalted butter, softened**

¾ **cup granulated sugar**

¾ **cup packed brown sugar**

2 **eggs**

1 **teaspoon baking soda**

1 **teaspoon vanilla**

2 **cups all-purpose flour**

1 **cup chunky peanut butter**

1 **cup semisweet or milk chocolate chips**

1 **cup peanut butter chips**

1. Preheat oven to 350°F. Line cookie sheets with parchment paper or lightly grease.

2. Beat butter and sugars in large bowl with electric mixer at medium speed until blended. Add eggs, baking soda and vanilla; beat until light. Add flour and peanut butter; beat at low speed until dough is stiff and smooth. Stir in chocolate and peanut butter chips.

3. Drop dough by heaping tablespoonfuls 2 inches apart onto prepared cookie sheets. Press cookies down with tines of fork to flatten slightly.

4. Bake 12 minutes or until set but not browned. *Do not overbake.* Remove to wire racks; cool completely.

OATMEAL CANDY CHIPPERS

Makes about 4 dozen cookies

2¾ cups old-fashioned or quick oats

¾ cup all-purpose flour

¾ teaspoon salt

½ teaspoon baking soda

¾ cup (1½ sticks) unsalted butter, softened

¾ cup granulated sugar

¾ cup packed brown sugar

1 egg

3 tablespoons milk

2 teaspoons vanilla

¾ cup candy-coated chocolate pieces

1. Preheat oven to 375°F. Line cookie sheets with parchment paper. Combine oats, flour, salt and baking soda in medium bowl.

2. Beat butter and sugars in large bowl with electric mixer at medium speed 3 to 4 minutes or until light and fluffy. Beat in egg, milk and vanilla until well blended. Gradually beat in flour mixture at low speed just until blended. Stir in chocolate pieces.

3. Drop dough by rounded tablespoonfuls 2 inches apart onto prepared cookie sheets.

4. Bake 10 to 12 minutes or until edges are golden brown. Cool cookies on cookie sheets 2 minutes. Remove to wire racks; cool completely.

EXTRA-CHOCOLATEY BROWNIE COOKIES

Makes about 4 dozen cookies

- 2 cups all-purpose flour
- ½ cup unsweetened Dutch process or natural cocoa powder
- 1 teaspoon baking soda
- ¾ teaspoon salt
- 1 cup (2 sticks) unsalted butter, softened
- 1 cup packed brown sugar
- ½ cup granulated sugar
- 2 eggs
- 2 teaspoons vanilla
- 1 package (10 to 12 ounces) semisweet chocolate chunks or chips
- 2 cups coarsely chopped walnuts or pecans

1. Preheat oven to 350°F. Whisk flour, cocoa, baking soda and salt in medium bowl until well blended.

2. Beat butter in large bowl with electric mixer at medium speed 1 minute or until creamy. Add sugars; beat 2 minutes or until light and fluffy. Add eggs and vanilla; beat until well blended. Gradually beat in flour mixture at low speed just until blended. Stir in chocolate chunks and walnuts.

3. Drop dough by heaping tablespoonfuls 2 inches apart onto ungreased cookie sheets; flatten slightly.

4. Bake 8 to 10 minutes or until set. Cool on cookie sheets 2 minutes. Remove to wire racks; cool completely.

PISTACHIO LEMON SHORTBREAD COOKIES

Makes 3 dozen cookies

1 cup (2 sticks) unsalted butter, softened

½ cup packed brown sugar

¼ cup powdered sugar

Grated peel of 1 lemon

½ teaspoon salt

½ teaspoon vanilla

2 cups all-purpose flour

1¼ cups coarsely chopped toasted* pistachios

½ cup white chocolate chips

*To toast nuts, spread in single layer on baking pan. Bake at 350°F 5 to 7 minutes or until lightly browned and fragrant. Cool before using.

1. Preheat oven to 300°F.

2. Beat butter and sugars in large bowl with electric mixer at medium-high speed 5 minutes or until light and fluffy. Add lemon peel, salt and vanilla; mix well. With mixer running on low speed, gradually add flour. Add pistachios and white chocolate chips; mix just until blended.

3. Shape dough by tablespoonfuls into 1-inch balls; place on ungreased cookie sheets. Flatten slightly.

4. Bake 15 minutes or until lightly browned around edges. Cool on cookie sheets 5 minutes. Remove to wire racks; cool completely.

ALL THE CHIPS COOKIES

Makes about 4 dozen cookies

2 cups old-fashioned oats

1⅓ cups all-purpose flour

¾ teaspoon baking soda

½ teaspoon baking powder

½ teaspoon salt

1 cup packed brown sugar

¾ cup (1½ sticks) unsalted butter, softened

¼ cup granulated sugar

1 egg

1 tablespoon honey

1 teaspoon vanilla

½ cup milk chocolate chips

½ cup white chocolate chips

½ cup semisweet chocolate chips

½ cup mini candy-coated chocolate pieces

½ cup chopped honey-roasted peanuts or peanut butter chips

1. Preheat oven to 350°F. Line cookie sheets with parchment paper. Combine oats, flour, baking soda, baking powder and salt in medium bowl.

2. Beat brown sugar, butter and granulated sugar in large bowl with electric mixer at medium speed until light and fluffy. Add egg, honey and vanilla; beat until well blended. Gradually beat in flour mixture at low speed just until blended. Stir in chocolate chips, candies and peanuts. Drop dough by rounded tablespoonfuls onto prepared cookie sheets.

3. Bake about 10 minutes or until cookies are puffed and golden. Cool on cookie sheets 5 minutes. Remove to wire racks; cool completely.

CLASSIC CHOCOLATE CHIP COOKIES

Makes about 2 dozen cookies

1¼ cups all-purpose flour

½ teaspoon salt

½ teaspoon baking soda

½ cup (1 stick) unsalted butter, softened

½ cup granulated sugar

¼ cup packed brown sugar

1 egg

1 teaspoon vanilla

1 cup semisweet or bittersweet chocolate chips

Coarse salt or flaky sea salt

1. Preheat oven to 350°F. Line cookie sheets with parchment paper. Whisk flour, ½ teaspoon salt and baking soda in medium bowl.

2. Beat butter and sugars in large bowl with electric mixer at medium speed 3 to 4 minutes or until light and fluffy. Add egg and vanilla; beat until well blended. Add flour mixture; beat just until blended. Stir in chocolate chips.

3. Drop tablespoonfuls of dough 2 inches apart onto prepared cookie sheets. Sprinkle tops with coarse salt.

4. Bake 10 to 12 minutes or until edges are lightly browned. Cool on cookie sheets 1 minute. Remove to wire racks; cool completely.

NOTE

For best flavor, wrap dough in plastic wrap and refrigerate overnight or up to 2 days.

GIANT COOKIES

HUGE CHOCOLATE CHIP WALNUT COOKIES

Makes 12 cookies

1¾ cups all-purpose flour

1 cup cake flour

1 teaspoon baking powder

¾ teaspoon baking soda

¾ teaspoon salt

1 cup (2 sticks) cold unsalted butter, cut into cubes

¾ cup packed brown sugar

½ cup granulated sugar

2 eggs

1 teaspoon vanilla

2 cups coarsely chopped walnuts

2 cups semisweet chocolate chips

1. Preheat oven to 400°F. Line cookie sheets with parchment paper. Position oven rack in center of oven. Whisk all-purpose flour, cake flour, baking powder, baking soda and salt in medium bowl.

2. Beat butter and sugars in large bowl with electric mixer at medium speed 1 to 2 minutes or until smooth and creamy. Add eggs, one at a time; beat until well blended. Beat in vanilla. Gradually beat in flour mixture at low speed just until blended. Stir in walnuts and chocolate chips until blended.

3. Shape dough into 12 mounds slightly smaller than a tennis ball (about 4 ounces each); arrange 2 inches apart on prepared cookie sheets (6 cookies per cookie sheet).

4. Bake one sheet at a time about 12 minutes or until tops are light golden brown. (Cover loosely with foil if cookies are browning too quickly.) Remove cookie sheet to wire rack; cool cookies on cookie sheet 15 minutes. (Cookies will continue to bake while standing.) Serve warm.

DOUBLE CHOCOLATE CRANBERRY CHUNKIES

Makes 12 cookies

1¾ **cups all-purpose flour**

⅓ **cup unsweetened cocoa powder**

½ **teaspoon baking powder**

½ **teaspoon salt**

1 **cup (2 sticks) unsalted butter, softened**

1 **cup granulated sugar, plus additional for flattening cookies**

½ **cup packed brown sugar**

1 **egg**

1 **teaspoon vanilla**

2 **cups semisweet chocolate chunks or large chocolate chips**

¾ **cup dried cranberries or dried tart cherries**

1. Preheat oven to 350°F. Whisk flour, cocoa, baking powder and salt in medium bowl.

2. Beat butter, 1 cup granulated sugar and brown sugar in large bowl with electric mixer at medium speed 3 to 4 minutes or until light and fluffy. Beat in egg and vanilla until well blended. Gradually beat in flour mixture at low speed just until blended. Stir in chocolate chunks and cranberries.

3. Drop dough by level ¼ cupfuls onto ungreased cookie sheets, spacing 3 inches apart. Flatten dough with bottom of glass that has been dipped in additional granulated sugar until 2½ inches in diameter.

4. Bake 11 to 12 minutes or until cookies are set. Cool 2 minutes on cookie sheets. Remove to wire racks; cool completely.

BLACK AND WHITE COOKIES

Makes 18 cookies

COOKIES

- 2 cups all-purpose flour
- 1 tablespoon cornstarch
- ¾ teaspoon baking soda
- ½ teaspoon salt
- ¾ cup (1½ sticks) unsalted butter, softened
- 1 cup granulated sugar
- 2 eggs
- 1 teaspoon vanilla
- ½ teaspoon grated lemon peel
- ⅔ cup buttermilk

ICINGS

- 3½ cups powdered sugar, divided
- 3 tablespoons plus 3 teaspoons boiling water, divided
- 1 tablespoon lemon juice
- 2 teaspoons corn syrup, divided
- ¼ teaspoon vanilla
- 3 ounces unsweetened chocolate, melted

1. Preheat oven to 350°F. Line cookie sheets with parchment paper. Whisk flour, cornstarch, baking soda and salt in medium bowl.

2. Beat butter and granulated sugar in large bowl with electric mixer at medium-high speed 3 to 4 minutes or until light and fluffy. Beat in eggs, one at a time; beat in 1 teaspoon vanilla and lemon peel. Add flour mixture alternately with buttermilk, beating at low speed until blended after each addition. Scrape bowl with rubber spatula and stir several times to bring dough together. Using dampened hands, shape 3 tablespoons dough into a ball for each cookie. Place 3 inches apart on prepared cookie sheets.

3. Bake 13 to 15 minutes or until tops are puffed and edges are lightly browned. Cool on cookie sheets 1 minute. Remove to wire racks; trim any crispy browned edges, if desired. Cool completely.

4. Place 2 cups powdered sugar in small bowl; whisk in 1 tablespoon boiling water, lemon juice and 1 teaspoon corn syrup until smooth and well blended. If necessary, add additional 1 teaspoon boiling water to make smooth, thick and spreadable glaze. Spread icing over half of each cookie; place on wire rack or waxed paper to set. Place remaining 1½ cups powdered sugar in another small bowl; whisk in 2 tablespoons boiling water, remaining 1 teaspoon corn syrup and ¼ teaspoon vanilla. Whisk in chocolate until smooth and well blended. If necessary, add additional 1 to 2 teaspoons boiling water to make smooth, thick and spreadable glaze. Spread icing on other side of each cookie. Place on wire rack; let stand until set. Cookies are best the day they're made, but they can be stored in airtight container at room temperature for 1 to 2 days.

WHITE CHOCOLATE BIGGIES

Makes about 2 dozen cookies

2½ **cups all-purpose flour**

⅔ **cup unsweetened cocoa powder**

1 **teaspoon baking soda**

½ **teaspoon salt**

1½ **cups (3 sticks) unsalted butter, softened**

1 **cup granulated sugar**

¾ **cup packed brown sugar**

2 **eggs**

2 **teaspoons vanilla**

1 **package (10 ounces) large white chocolate chips *or* 10 ounces white chocolate bar, coarsely chopped**

¾ **cup pecan halves, coarsely chopped**

½ **cup golden raisins**

1. Preheat oven to 350°F. Lightly grease cookie sheets or line with parchment paper. Whisk flour, cocoa, baking soda and salt in medium bowl.

2. Beat butter and sugars in large bowl with electric mixer at medium speed 3 to 4 minutes or until light and fluffy. Add eggs, one at a time; beat in vanilla. Gradually beat in flour mixture at low speed just until blended. Stir in white chocolate chips, pecans and raisins.

3. Drop dough by ⅓ cupfuls about 4 inches apart onto prepared cookie sheets. Flatten slightly with fingertips.

4. Bake 12 to 14 minutes or until firm in center. Cool 5 minutes on cookie sheets. Remove to wire racks; cool completely.

CHOCOLATE CHUNK PIZZA COOKIE

Makes 3 pizza cookies (2 to 3 servings each)

2 cups all-purpose flour

1 teaspoon baking soda

1 teaspoon salt

¾ cup (1½ sticks) unsalted butter, softened

1 cup packed brown sugar

¼ cup granulated sugar

2 eggs

1 teaspoon vanilla

1 package (about 11 ounces) chocolate chunks

Vanilla ice cream

1. Preheat oven to 400°F. Spray three 6-inch cast iron skillets, cake pans or deep-dish pizza pans with nonstick cooking spray.*

2. Whisk flour, baking soda and salt in medium bowl. Beat butter and sugars in large bowl with electric mixer at medium speed until creamy. Beat in eggs and vanilla until well blended. Gradually beat in flour mixture at low speed just until blended. Stir in chocolate chunks. Spread dough evenly in prepared pans.

3. Bake about 15 minutes or until top and edges are deep golden brown but center is still slightly soft. Top with ice cream. Serve warm.

If you don't have three skillets or pans, you can bake one cookie at a time. Refrigerate the dough between batches and make sure the skillet is completely cool before adding more dough. (Clean and spray the skillet again before adding each new batch.)

CHOCOLATE COOKIE POPS

Makes 16 cookies

2 cups all-purpose flour

½ cup unsweetened cocoa powder

½ teaspoon baking powder

½ teaspoon salt

1 cup (2 sticks) unsalted butter, softened

1 cup granulated sugar, plus additional for flattening cookies

½ cup packed brown sugar

1 egg

1 teaspoon vanilla

½ cup semisweet chocolate chips

½ cup white chocolate chips or chopped white chocolate candy bar

1 teaspoon shortening, divided

Sprinkles and decors

1. Preheat oven to 350°F. Whisk flour, cocoa, baking powder and salt in medium bowl.

2. Beat butter, 1 cup granulated sugar and brown sugar in large bowl with electric mixer at medium-high speed 3 to 4 minutes or until light and fluffy. Beat in egg and vanilla until well blended. Gradually beat in flour mixture at low speed just until blended.

3. Drop dough by scant ¼ cupfuls 3 inches apart onto ungreased or parchment-lined cookie sheets. Dip bottom of glass in granulated sugar; flatten cookies until 2 inches in diameter. Insert wooden pop stick 1½ inches into each cookie.

4. Bake 14 to 16 minutes or until cookies are set. Cool on cookie sheets 10 minutes. If necessary, trim uneven crispy edges from cookies with sharp knife. Remove to wire racks; cool completely.

5. Combine semisweet chocolate chips and ½ teaspoon shortening in small microwavable bowl. Microwave on HIGH 30 seconds; stir. Continue microwaving at 10-second intervals until melted and smooth. Repeat with white chocolate chips and remaining ½ teaspoon shortening. Place glazes in small resealable food storage bags with small corners cut off. Pipe in spiral shape on cookies; sprinkle with decors. Let stand until set.

TIP

Instead of using wooden pop sticks, try colorful paper straws instead. Bake cookies without sticks and immediately remove to wire racks. Carefully insert a straw into each hot cookie all the way to the top.

⇒ SPICY GINGER MOLASSES COOKIES ⇐

Makes about 12 cookies

2 cups all-purpose flour

1½ teaspoons ground ginger

1 teaspoon baking soda

½ teaspoon ground cloves

¼ teaspoon salt

¾ cup (1½ sticks) unsalted butter, softened

1 cup sugar, plus additional for flattening cookies

¼ cup molasses

1 egg

½ cup white chocolate- or yogurt-covered raisins

1. Preheat oven to 375°F. Line cookie sheets with parchment paper. Whisk flour, ginger, baking soda, cloves and salt in medium bowl.

2. Beat butter and 1 cup sugar in large bowl with electric mixer at medium speed 3 to 4 minutes or until light and fluffy. Add molasses and egg; beat until well blended. Gradually beat in flour mixture at low speed just until blended.

3. Drop dough by level ¼ cupfuls about 3 inches apart onto prepared cookie sheets; flatten with bottom of glass dipped in additional sugar until about 2 inches in diameter. Press 8 to 9 white chocolate-covered raisins into dough of each cookie.

4. Bake 11 to 12 minutes or until cookies are set. Cool on cookie sheets 2 minutes; slide parchment paper and cookies onto wire racks. Cool completely.

CHOCOLATE-COCONUT-TOFFEE DELIGHTS

Makes 12 cookies

½ cup all-purpose flour

½ teaspoon salt

¼ teaspoon baking powder

1 package (12 ounces) semisweet chocolate chips, divided

¼ cup (½ stick) unsalted butter, cut into small pieces

¾ cup packed brown sugar

2 eggs

1 teaspoon vanilla

1½ cups flaked coconut

1 cup toffee baking bits

½ cup bittersweet chocolate chips

1. Preheat oven to 350°F. Line cookie sheets with parchment paper. Whisk flour, salt and baking powder in small bowl.

2. Combine 1 cup semisweet chocolate chips and butter in medium microwavable bowl. Microwave on HIGH 1 minute; stir. Microwave at additional 30-second intervals until mixture is melted and smooth, stirring after each interval.

3. Beat brown sugar, eggs and vanilla in large bowl with electric mixer at medium speed until creamy. Beat in chocolate mixture until well blended. Add flour mixture; beat at low speed until blended. Stir in coconut, toffee bits and remaining 1 cup semisweet chocolate chips. Drop dough by heaping ⅓ cupfuls 3 inches apart onto prepared cookie sheets. Flatten with spatula into 3½-inch circles.

4. Bake 15 to 17 minutes or until edges are firm to the touch. Cool on cookie sheets 2 minutes; slide parchment paper and cookies onto wire racks to cool completely.

5. For chocolate drizzle, place bittersweet chocolate chips in small microwavable bowl. Microwave on HIGH 30 seconds; stir. Microwave at additional 30-second intervals until melted and smooth, stirring after each interval. Drizzle over cookies with fork. Let stand until set.

PEANUT BUTTER JUMBOS

Makes 2 dozen cookies

1 **cup peanut butter**

⅔ **cup granulated sugar**

⅔ **cup packed brown sugar**

⅓ **cup unsalted butter, softened**

2 **eggs**

1 **teaspoon vanilla**

3 **cups old-fashioned oats**

1½ **teaspoons baking soda**

½ **teaspoon salt**

⅔ **cup mini candy-coated chocolate pieces**

⅔ **cup semisweet chocolate chips**

1. Preheat oven to 350°F. Grease cookie sheets or line with parchment paper.

2. Beat peanut butter, sugars and butter in large bowl with electric mixer at medium speed until smooth. Beat in eggs and vanilla until well blended. Stir in oats, baking soda and salt just until blended. Stir in chocolate pieces and chocolate chips.

3. Drop dough by ¼ cupfuls 4 inches apart onto prepared cookie sheets. Flatten slightly.

4. Bake 12 to 15 minutes or until firm in center. *Do not overbake.* Cool on cookie sheets 1 minute. Remove to wire racks; cool completely.

DARK CHOCOLATE DREAMS

Makes 14 cookies

½ **cup all-purpose flour**

1 **teaspoon instant espresso powder** *or* ¼ **teaspoon ground cinnamon**

½ **teaspoon baking powder**

½ **teaspoon salt**

16 **ounces bittersweet chocolate, coarsely chopped**

¼ **cup (½ stick) butter**

1½ **cups sugar**

3 **eggs**

1 **teaspoon vanilla**

1 **package (12 ounces) white chocolate chips**

1 **cup dark chocolate chips**

1. Preheat oven to 350°F. Line cookie sheets with parchment paper. Whisk flour, espresso powder, baking powder and salt in small bowl.

2. Combine chocolate and butter in medium heavy saucepan. Heat over low heat until mixture is melted and smooth, stirring constantly. Or microwave in microwavable bowl on HIGH 2 minutes; stir. Microwave 1 to 2 minutes, stirring after 1 minute, or until chocolate is melted. Cool slightly.

3. Beat sugar, eggs and vanilla with electric mixer at medium-high speed about 6 minutes or until very thick and mixture is pale. Reduce speed to low; slowly beat in chocolate mixture until well blended. Gradually beat in flour mixture until blended. Fold in white chocolate chips and dark chocolate chips.

4. Drop dough by level ⅓ cupfuls 3 inches apart onto prepared cookie sheets. Flatten dough into 4-inch circles with moistened fingers.

5. Bake 12 minutes or just until firm and surface begins to crack. *Do not overbake.* Cool on cookie sheets 2 minutes. Remove to wire racks; cool completely.

SUGAR & SPICE

NUTMEG MOLASSES COOKIES

Makes about 5 dozen cookies

- 3 **cups all-purpose flour**
- 2 **teaspoons baking soda**
- 1 **teaspoon ground nutmeg**
- 1 **teaspoon ground cinnamon**
- ½ **teaspoon salt**
- 1½ **cups sugar, plus additional for flattening cookies**
- 1 **cup shortening**
- ⅓ **cup molasses**
- 1 **teaspoon vanilla**
- 2 **eggs**

1. Preheat oven to 350°F. Whisk flour, baking soda, nutmeg, cinnamon and salt in medium bowl.

2. Beat 1½ cups sugar, shortening, molasses and vanilla in large bowl with electric mixer at medium speed until creamy. Add eggs, one at a time, beating well after each addition. Gradually beat in flour mixture at low speed just until blended. Beat at medium speed until thick dough forms.

3. Shape dough into 1½-inch balls. Place 3 inches apart on ungreased cookie sheets. Flatten with bottom of glass dipped in additional sugar.

4. Bake 10 minutes or until cookies look dry. Cool on cookie sheets 2 minutes. Remove to wire racks; cool completely.

GINGER SHORTBREAD DELIGHTS

Makes about 3½ dozen cookies

1 cup (2 sticks) plus
   2 tablespoons unsalted
   butter, softened, divided

½ cup plus 1 tablespoon
   powdered sugar, divided

⅓ cup packed brown sugar

½ teaspoon plus ⅛ teaspoon
   salt, divided

2 cups minus 2 tablespoons
   all-purpose flour

4 ounces crystallized ginger

1 bar (3 to 3½ ounces)
   bittersweet chocolate,
   broken into small pieces

2 tablespoons whipping
   cream

1. Preheat oven to 300°F.

2. Beat 1 cup butter, ½ cup powdered sugar, brown sugar and ½ teaspoon salt in large bowl with electric mixer at medium speed until creamy. Gradually beat in flour at low speed just until well blended.

3. Shape dough by tablespoons into balls. Place 1 inch apart on ungreased cookie sheets; flatten to ½-inch thickness. Cut ginger into ¼-inch-thick slices. Place 1 ginger slice on top of each cookie.

4. Bake 20 minutes or until set and lightly browned. Cool on cookie sheets 5 minutes. Remove to wire racks; cool completely.

5. For glaze, melt chocolate and remaining 2 tablespoons butter in small heavy saucepan over very low heat, stirring constantly. Remove from heat. Add cream, remaining 1 tablespoon powdered sugar and remaining ⅛ teaspoon salt; stir until smooth. Drizzle over cookies. Let stand about 30 minutes or until glaze is set.

HONEY SPICE BALLS

Makes about 2½ dozen cookies

½ **cup (1 stick) unsalted butter, softened**

½ **cup packed brown sugar**

1 **egg**

1 **tablespoon honey**

1 **teaspoon vanilla**

½ **teaspoon baking powder**

½ **teaspoon ground cinnamon**

½ **teaspoon salt**

¼ **teaspoon ground nutmeg**

2 **cups all-purpose flour**

½ **cup quick oats**

1. Preheat oven to 350°F. Grease cookie sheets or line with parchment paper.

2. Beat butter and brown sugar in large bowl with electric mixer at medium speed until creamy. Add egg, honey and vanilla; beat until light and fluffy. Add baking powder, cinnamon, salt and nutmeg. Gradually beat in flour at low speed just until blended.

3. Place oats in small bowl. Shape tablespoonfuls of dough into balls; roll in oats. Place 2 inches apart on prepared cookie sheets.

4. Bake 15 to 18 minutes or until cookie tops crack slightly. Cool on cookie sheets 1 minute. Remove to wire racks; cool completely.

CHEWY PECAN GINGERSNAP TRIANGLES

Makes 2 dozen triangles

20 gingersnap cookies, broken in half

½ cup (1 stick) unsalted butter, softened

¼ cup granulated sugar

¼ cup packed brown sugar

1 egg, separated

½ teaspoon vanilla

¼ teaspoon salt

1 teaspoon water

1½ cups chopped pecan pieces (6 ounces)

1. Preheat oven to 350°F. Line bottom and sides of 13×9-inch baking pan with foil, leaving 2-inch overhang. Spray foil with nonstick cooking spray.

2. Place gingersnap cookies in food processor; process until crumbs form. (Or place cookies in resealable food storage bag and crush with rolling pin or meat mallet.)

3. Beat butter, sugars, egg yolk and vanilla in medium bowl with electric mixer at medium speed until well blended. Add cookie crumbs and salt; mix well. Lightly press crumb mixture into bottom of prepared pan to form thin crust.

4. Whisk egg white and water in small bowl. Brush mixture evenly over crust; sprinkle evenly with pecans, pressing lightly to adhere.

5. Bake 20 minutes or until lightly browned. Cool completely in pan on wire rack. Use foil handles to remove bars from pan to cutting board. Cut into 3-inch squares; cut squares diagonally in half.

OLD WORLD PFEFFERNÜSSE COOKIES

Makes about 4 dozen cookies

- ¾ cup packed brown sugar
- ½ cup (1 stick) unsalted butter, softened
- ½ cup molasses
- 1 egg
- 1 tablespoon licorice-flavored liqueur (optional)
- 3¼ cups all-purpose flour
- 1 teaspoon baking soda
- 1 teaspoon ground cinnamon
- ½ teaspoon salt
- ½ teaspoon ground cloves
- ¼ teaspoon ground nutmeg
- Dash black pepper

1. Preheat oven to 350°F. Lightly grease cookie sheets or line with parchment paper.

2. Beat brown sugar and butter in large bowl with electric mixer until creamy. Beat in molasses, egg and liqueur, if desired, until light and fluffy. Add flour, baking soda, cinnamon, salt, cloves, nutmeg and pepper; beat at low speed just until blended. Shape level tablespoonfuls of dough into balls. Place 2 inches apart on prepared cookie sheets.

3. Bake 12 to 14 minutes or until set. Cool on baking sheet 2 minutes. Remove to wire racks; cool completely.

CHOCOLATE-DIPPED CINNAMON THINS

Makes about 2 dozen cookies

1¼ **cups all-purpose flour**

1½ **teaspoons ground cinnamon**

½ **teaspoon salt**

1 **cup (2 sticks) unsalted butter, softened**

1 **cup powdered sugar**

1 **egg**

1 **teaspoon vanilla**

4 **ounces chopped bittersweet chocolate, melted**

1. Combine flour, cinnamon and salt in small bowl. Beat butter in large bowl with electric mixer at medium speed until creamy. Add powdered sugar; beat until well blended. Beat in egg and vanilla. Gradually beat in flour mixture just until blended.

2. Place dough on sheet of waxed paper. Using waxed paper to hold dough, roll back and forth to form log about 2½ inches in diameter and 12 inches long. Securely wrap log in plastic wrap. Refrigerate at least 2 hours or until firm. (Log may be frozen up to 3 months; thaw in refrigerator before baking.)

3. Preheat oven to 350°F. Cut dough into ¼-inch-thick slices. Place 2 inches apart on ungreased cookie sheets. Bake 10 minutes or until set. Cool on cookie sheets 2 minutes. Remove to wire racks; cool completely.

4. Dip half of each cookie into melted chocolate. Place on waxed paper; let stand at room temperature about 40 minutes or until chocolate is set.

5. Store cookies between sheets of waxed paper at room temperature or in refrigerator.

GINGER SPICE THUMBPRINTS

Makes about 4 dozen cookies

2¼ cups all-purpose flour

1¾ teaspoons ground ginger

1½ teaspoons ground cinnamon

1 teaspoon baking soda

¼ teaspoon salt

¾ cup packed brown sugar

½ cup (1 stick) unsalted butter, softened

¼ cup molasses

1 egg

Granulated sugar

½ cup apricot, fig or any flavor preserves

1. Preheat oven to 350°F. Lightly grease cookie sheets or line with parchment paper. Whisk flour, ginger, cinnamon, baking soda and salt in medium bowl.

2. Beat brown sugar and butter in large bowl with electric mixer at medium speed until well blended. Add molasses and egg; beat until well blended. Gradually beat in flour mixture at low speed just until blended.

3. Place granulated sugar in shallow bowl. Shape dough into 1-inch balls; roll in sugar to coat. Place 1½ inches apart on prepared cookie sheets. Press center of each ball with thumb; fill each indentation with ½ teaspoon preserves.

4. Bake 13 minutes or until edges are lightly browned. Cool on cookie sheets 1 minute. Remove to wire racks; cool completely.

GINGER MOLASSES THINS

Makes about 2½ dozen cookies

1¼ cups all-purpose flour

1½ teaspoons ground ginger

½ teaspoon salt

½ teaspoon baking soda

½ teaspoon ground cinnamon

⅛ teaspoon ground cloves

½ cup (1 stick) butter, softened

½ cup packed light brown sugar

¼ cup granulated sugar

1 egg

2 tablespoons molasses

1 teaspoon vanilla

Coarse white decorating sugar

1. Preheat oven to 350°F. Lightly grease cookie sheets or line with parchment paper. Whisk flour, ginger, salt, baking soda, cinnamon and cloves in medium bowl.

2. Beat butter, brown sugar and granulated sugar in large bowl with electric mixer at medium speed until light and fluffy. Add egg, molasses and vanilla; beat until well blended. Gradually beat in flour mixture at low speed just until blended.

3. Place decorating sugar in small bowl. Shape dough by level tablespoons into balls; roll in sugar to coat. Place 2 inches apart on prepared cookie sheets.

4. Bake about 10 minutes or until edges are lightly browned. Cool on cookie sheets 1 minute. Remove to wire racks; cool completely.

CARDAMOM SHORTBREAD

Makes 16 large cookies

- 2 cups all-purpose flour
- 1 teaspoon ground cardamom
- ½ teaspoon baking powder
- ½ teaspoon salt
- ¾ cup (1½ sticks) unsalted butter
- ¼ cup powdered sugar
- 3 tablespoons honey
- 16 whole cardamom pods (optional)
- 3 teaspoons granulated sugar

1. Preheat oven to 300°F. Whisk flour, ground cardamom, baking powder and salt in medium bowl.

2. Beat butter, powdered sugar and honey in large bowl with electric mixer at medium speed until light and fluffy. Add flour mixture; beat on low speed until mixture resembles coarse crumbs.

3. Transfer dough to lightly floured surface. Knead 10 times; divide in half. Working with one half at a time, shape dough into a ball.

4. Place dough between two sheets of parchment paper; roll into 8-inch circle. Remove top piece of parchment; place dough on ungreased cookie sheet. Trim dough to make perfect circle (place 8-inch plate or bowl on dough and trim around edge). Score dough into eight wedges. Press whole cardamom seeds into wedges, if desired. Sprinkle evenly with granulated sugar.

5. Bake 20 to 25 minutes or until golden brown. Remove shortbread and parchment to wire racks; cool 10 minutes. Transfer to cutting board; cut along scored lines.

DARK COCOA SPICE COOKIES

Makes about 5 dozen cookies

2½ **cups all-purpose flour**

½ **cup unsweetened Dutch process or natural cocoa powder**

1 **teaspoon ground cinnamon**

1 **teaspoon ground cardamom**

½ **teaspoon baking soda**

¼ **teaspoon salt**

1½ **cups packed dark brown sugar**

1 **cup (2 sticks) unsalted butter, softened**

2 **egg yolks**

1 **teaspoon vanilla**

Demerara sugar or coarse decorating sugar

1. Whisk flour, cocoa, cinnamon, cardamom, baking soda and salt in medium bowl.

2. Beat brown sugar and butter in large bowl with electric mixer at medium speed until light and fluffy. Beat in egg yolks and vanilla. Gradually beat in flour mixture at low speed just until blended.

3. Spread demerara sugar evenly on waxed paper. Divide dough into four pieces; shape each piece into 6-inch log. Roll logs in sugar, coating evenly. Wrap in plastic wrap and refrigerate 3 to 4 hours or until firm.

4. Preheat oven to 325°F. Line cookie sheets with parchment paper. Cut each log into 16 slices; place 1 inch apart on prepared cookie sheets.

5. Bake 12 minutes. Cool on cookie sheets 5 minutes. Remove to wire racks; cool completely.

CHOCOLATEY BITES

CHOCOLATE PRETZEL COOKIES

Makes 4 dozen cookies

- **1 cup (2 sticks) unsalted butter, softened**
- **¾ cup granulated sugar**
- **½ cup unsweetened cocoa powder**
- **1 egg**
- **1 teaspoon vanilla**
- **2 cups cake flour**
- **1 teaspoon coarse salt, plus additional for garnish**
- **4 ounces white chocolate, chopped**
- **Pearl sugar**

1. Beat butter and granulated sugar in large bowl with electric mixer at medium-high speed 3 to 4 minutes or until light and fluffy. Add cocoa, egg and vanilla; beat until well blended. Stir in flour and 1 teaspoon salt until well blended. Shape dough into a disc; wrap in plastic wrap. Refrigerate 1 hour or until firm.

2. Preheat oven to 350°F. Line cookie sheets with parchment paper. Roll tablespoonfuls of dough into 12-inch ropes; shape into pretzels and place on prepared cookie sheets 2 inches apart. Bake 7 to 8 minutes or until firm. Cool on cookie sheets 5 minutes. Remove to wire racks; cool completely.

3. Place cookies on parchment paper. Melt white chocolate according to package directions. Drizzle over cookies; sprinkle with additional salt and pearl sugar. Let stand until set.

⇒ CHOCOLATE CARAMEL PECAN THUMBPRINTS ⇐

Makes about 2½ dozen cookies

1½ cups all-purpose flour

¾ cup unsweetened cocoa powder

1 cup (2 sticks) unsalted butter, softened

⅔ cup packed brown sugar

½ teaspoon salt

2 eggs, separated

1 teaspoon vanilla

2 cups pecan halves, finely chopped

CARAMEL FILLING

½ cup packed brown sugar

¼ cup (½ stick) unsalted butter

Pinch of salt

2 tablespoons whipping cream

2 tablespoons powdered sugar

1. Preheat oven to 350°F. Line cookie sheets with parchment paper. Whisk flour and cocoa in small bowl until well blended.

2. Beat 1 cup butter, ⅔ cup brown sugar and ½ teaspoon salt in large bowl with electric mixer at medium speed until light and fluffy. Beat in egg yolks and vanilla until well blended. Gradually beat in flour mixture at low speed just until blended.

3. Shape dough by tablespoonfuls into 1-inch balls. Place egg whites in small bowl; place pecans in medium bowl. Working with 2 to 3 at a time, dip dough balls into egg whites, letting excess drip back into bowl. Roll in nuts to coat completely; place 2 inches apart on prepared cookie sheets. Press thumb into center of each cookie to form indentation.

4. Bake 10 minutes or until cookies are set and no longer shiny. Quickly repress thumbprints with end of wooden spoon. Remove to wire racks; cool completely.

5. For filling, combine ½ cup brown sugar, ¼ cup butter and pinch of salt in small saucepan. Cook over medium heat until mixture boils, stirring constantly. Boil 1 minute, stirring constantly. Remove from heat; stir in cream. Cool 15 minutes. Whisk in powdered sugar until smooth and well blended. Fill each cookie with about ½ teaspoon filling. Let stand until filling is set.

ROCKY ROAD CRISPY TREATS

Makes 2 to 3 dozen treats

- 6 **tablespoons butter**
- 2 **packages (10 ounces each) large marshmallows**
- 1 **package (12 ounces) semisweet chocolate chips, divided**
- 12 **cups crisp rice cereal (one 13½-ounce box)**
- 1 **package (6 ounces) sliced almonds (1⅔ cups), divided**
- 2 **cups mini marshmallows**

1. Spray 13×9-inch baking pan with nonstick cooking spray.

2. Melt butter in large saucepan over low heat. Add large marshmallows; stir until completely melted. Stir in 1 cup chocolate chips until melted. Remove saucepan from heat; stir in cereal until well coated. Add remaining 1 cup chocolate chips, 1 cup almonds and mini marshmallows; stir to distribute evenly.

3. Press mixture into prepared pan with buttered hands, pressing down firmly to form even layer. Sprinkle with remaining ⅔ cup almonds. Cool completely before cutting. Serve immediately or store in airtight container up to 1 day.

⇉ CHOCOLATE PINWHEELS ⇇

Makes 40 cookies

- **1 cup (2 sticks) unsalted butter, softened**
- **½ cup powdered sugar**
- **2 tablespoons packed brown sugar**
- **½ teaspoon salt**
- **2 cups all-purpose flour**
- **¼ cup semisweet chocolate chips, melted**
- **1 tablespoon unsweetened cocoa powder**

1. Beat butter, sugars and salt in large bowl with electric mixer at medium speed 2 minutes or until light and fluffy. Add flour, ½ cup at a time, beating well after each addition. Remove half of dough; shape into a ball and wrap with plastic wrap. Add melted chocolate and cocoa to dough in bowl; beat just until blended. Shape chocolate dough into a ball; wrap in plastic wrap. Refrigerate both doughs at least 1 hour.

2. Divide chocolate and plain doughs in half. Roll out half of plain dough into 12×6-inch rectangle on lightly floured surface; transfer to sheet of parchment paper or plastic wrap. Roll half of chocolate dough into 12×6-inch rectangle on lightly floured surface; place over plain dough. Tightly roll up, starting at wide end, to form 12-inch log. If dough crumbles or breaks, press back together and continue to roll. Wrap in plastic wrap; refrigerate 1 hour. Repeat with remaining dough.

3. Preheat oven to 300°F. Cut each log into 20 slices; place on ungreased cookie sheets. Bake 13 to 15 minutes or until cookies are set and lightly browned. Cool on cookie sheets 5 minutes. Remove to wire racks; cool completely.

CHOCOLATE RASPBERRY THUMBPRINTS

Makes about 4 dozen cookies

1½ **cups (3 sticks) unsalted butter, softened**

1 **cup granulated sugar**

1 **egg**

1 **teaspoon vanilla**

3 **cups all-purpose flour**

¼ **cup unsweetened cocoa powder**

½ **teaspoon salt**

1 **cup mini semisweet chocolate chips (optional)**

⅔ **cup raspberry preserves**

Powdered sugar (optional)

1. Preheat oven to 350°F. Grease cookie sheets or line with parchment paper.

2. Beat butter and granulated sugar in large bowl with electric mixer at medium speed 3 to 4 minutes or until light and fluffy. Beat in egg and vanilla until light and fluffy. Mix in flour, cocoa and salt on low speed until well blended. Stir in mini chocolate chips, if desired.

3. Shape level tablespoonfuls of dough into balls. Place 2 inches apart on prepared cookie sheets. Make deep indentation in center of each ball with thumb.

4. Bake 12 to 15 minutes until just set. Cool on cookie sheets 2 minutes. Remove to wire racks; cool completely.

5. Fill centers with raspberry preserves and sprinkle with powdered sugar, if desired. Store between layers of waxed paper in airtight containers in refrigerator.

MEXICAN CHOCOLATE MACAROONS

Makes about 2 dozen cookies

8 ounces semisweet chocolate, divided

1¾ cups plus ⅓ cup whole almonds, divided

¾ cup sugar

½ teaspoon salt

2 egg whites

1 teaspoon ground cinnamon

1 teaspoon vanilla

1. Preheat oven to 400°F. Grease cookie sheets or line with parchment paper.

2. Place 5 ounces of chocolate in food processor; pulse until coarsely chopped. Add 1¾ cups almonds, sugar and salt; pulse until mixture is finely ground. Add egg whites, cinnamon and vanilla; process just until mixture forms moist dough.

3. Shape dough into 1-inch balls. (Dough will be sticky.) Place 2 inches apart on prepared cookie sheets. Press 1 whole almond into center of each dough ball.

4. Bake 8 to 10 minutes or just until set. Cool on cookie sheets 2 minutes. Remove to wire racks; cool completely.

5. Melt remaining 3 ounces of chocolate. Place in small resealable food storage bag. Cut off small corner of bag. Drizzle chocolate over cookies. Let stand until set.

DEEP DARK CHOCOLATE CHIP COOKIES

Makes about 2½ dozen cookies

- **2 packages (12 ounces each) semisweet chocolate chips, divided**
- **½ cup (1 stick) unsalted butter, cut into chunks**
- **2 eggs**
- **1 teaspoon vanilla**
- **¾ cup plus 2 tablespoons sugar**
- **⅔ cup all-purpose flour**
- **2 tablespoons unsweetened Dutch process or natural cocoa powder**
- **1 teaspoon baking powder**
- **½ teaspoon salt**

1. Lightly grease cookie sheets or line with parchment paper.

2. Combine 1 package (2 cups) chocolate chips and butter in large microwavable bowl. Microwave on HIGH 30 seconds; stir. Repeat as necessary until chips are melted and mixture is smooth. Let cool slightly.

3. Beat eggs and vanilla in large bowl with electric mixer at medium speed until blended and frothy. Add sugar; beat until thick and light. Add chocolate mixture; beat until blended. Add flour, cocoa, baking powder and salt; beat until blended. Stir in remaining chocolate chips. (Dough will be soft.)

4. Drop dough by rounded tablespoonfuls 1½ inches apart onto prepared cookie sheets. Refrigerate 30 minutes.

5. Preheat oven to 325°F. Bake 16 to 20 minutes or until cookies are firm to the touch. Cool on cookie sheets 2 minutes. Remove to wire racks; cool completely.

FUDGE BLOSSOMS

Makes about 2½ dozen cookies

- ½ cup (1 stick) unsalted butter, softened
- ¾ cup sugar
- 1 egg
- 1 teaspoon vanilla
- ½ teaspoon salt
- 1½ cups all-purpose flour
- ½ cup unsweetened cocoa powder
- ¾ to 1 cup finely chopped walnuts
- 48 chocolate star candies or unwrapped chocolate kisses

1. Beat butter and sugar in large bowl with electric mixer at medium speed until light and fluffy. Add egg, vanilla and salt; beat until well blended. Add flour and cocoa; beat at low speed just until blended. Shape dough into a ball; wrap in plastic wrap and refrigerate 1 hour or until firm.

2. Preheat oven to 350°F. Line cookie sheets with parchment paper. Place walnuts in small bowl. Shape dough into ½-inch balls. Roll in walnuts; press gently into dough. Place 2 inches apart on prepared cookie sheets.

3. Bake 12 minutes or until puffed and nearly set. Place chocolate star in center of each cookie; bake 1 minute. Cool on cookie sheets 2 minutes. Remove to wire racks; cool completely.

BROWNIES & BARS

SHORTBREAD TURTLE COOKIE BARS

Makes about 4 dozen bars

1¼ cups (2½ sticks) unsalted butter, softened, divided

1 cup all-purpose flour

1 cup old-fashioned oats

1¼ cups packed brown sugar, divided

1 teaspoon ground cinnamon

½ teaspoon salt

1½ cups chopped pecans

6 ounces bittersweet or semisweet chocolate, finely chopped

4 ounces white chocolate, finely chopped

1. Preheat oven to 350°F.

2. Beat ½ cup butter with electric mixer at medium speed 2 minutes or until light and fluffy. Add flour, oats, ¾ cup brown sugar, cinnamon and salt; beat at low speed until coarse crumbs form. Press firmly into ungreased 13×9-inch baking pan.

3. Combine remaining ¾ cup butter and ¾ cup brown sugar in medium saucepan. Cook over medium heat until mixture comes to a boil, stirring constantly. Boil 1 minute without stirring. Remove from heat; stir in pecans. Pour evenly over crust.

4. Bake 18 to 22 minutes or until caramel begins to bubble. Immediately sprinkle with bittersweet and white chocolate; swirl (do not spread) with knife after 45 seconds to 1 minute or when slightly softened. Cool completely in pan on wire rack. Cut into 2×1-inch bars.

TOFFEE LATTE NUT BARS

Makes 2 to 3 dozen bars

1½ **cups all-purpose flour**

¼ **cup powdered sugar**

½ **teaspoon salt**

¾ **cup (1½ sticks) cold unsalted butter, cut into pieces**

2 **teaspoons instant coffee granules**

1 **teaspoon hot water**

1 **can (14 ounces) sweetened condensed milk**

1 **egg**

1 **teaspoon vanilla**

1 **package (8 ounces) toffee baking bits**

1 **cup chopped walnuts or pecans**

¾ **cup flaked coconut** *or* **1 cup large coconut flakes**

1. Preheat oven to 350°F. Line 13×9-inch pan with parchment paper or spray with nonstick cooking spray.

2. Combine flour, powdered sugar and salt in large bowl. Add butter; mix with electric mixer at low speed until mixture resembles coarse crumbs. Or cut in butter with pastry blender. Press into prepared pan. Bake 15 minutes or until lightly browned around edges.

3. Meanwhile, dissolve coffee granules in hot water in large bowl. Whisk in condensed milk. Whisk in egg and vanilla until well blended. Stir in toffee bits and walnuts. Pour over crust; sprinkle with coconut.

4. Bake 25 minutes or until filling is set and coconut is toasted. Cool 5 minutes then loosen edges by running knife around sides of pan. Cool completely in pan on wire rack. Lift from pan using parchment; cut into bars.

BUTTERSCOTCH BROWNIES

Makes 16 brownies

1 cup butterscotch chips

1 cup all-purpose flour

½ teaspoon baking powder

¼ teaspoon salt

½ cup packed brown sugar

¼ cup (½ stick) unsalted butter, softened

2 eggs

½ teaspoon vanilla

1 cup semisweet chocolate chips

Unsweetened cocoa powder (optional)

1. Preheat oven to 350°F. Grease 9-inch square baking pan. Melt butterscotch chips in small saucepan over low heat, stirring constantly.

2. Combine flour, baking powder and salt in small bowl; add to butter mixture. Beat brown sugar and butter in large bowl with electric mixer at medium speed until light and fluffy. Beat in eggs, one at a time, scraping down side of bowl after each addition. Beat in melted butterscotch chips and vanilla. Beat until well blended. Spread batter evenly in prepared pan.

3. Bake 20 to 25 minutes or until golden brown and center is set. Immediately sprinkle with chocolate chips. Let stand about 4 minutes or until chocolate is melted. Spread chocolate evenly over top. Place pan on wire rack; cool completely. Sprinkle with cocoa, if desired. Cut into squares.

DOUBLE CHOCOLATE DREAM BARS

Makes 2 to 3 dozen bars

2¼ **cups all-purpose flour, divided**

1 **cup (2 sticks) unsalted butter, softened**

¾ **cup powdered sugar, plus additional for garnish**

⅓ **cup unsweetened cocoa powder**

½ **teaspoon salt**

2 **cups granulated sugar**

4 **eggs**

4 **ounces unsweetened chocolate, melted**

1. Preheat oven to 350°F. Line 13×9-inch baking pan with parchment paper.

2. Beat 2 cups flour, butter, ¾ cup powdered sugar, cocoa and salt in large bowl with electric mixer at low speed until blended. Beat at medium speed until well blended and stiff dough forms. Press firmly into prepared pan. Bake 15 to 20 minutes or just until set. *Do not overbake.*

3. Meanwhile, combine remaining ¼ cup flour and granulated sugar in large bowl. Add eggs and melted chocolate; beat with electric mixer at medium-high speed until well blended. Pour over crust.

4. Bake 25 minutes or until center is firm to the touch. Cool completely in pan on wire rack. Sprinkle with additional powdered sugar, if desired. Cut into bars.

PUMPKIN SWIRL BROWNIES

Makes about 16 brownies

PUMPKIN SWIRL

- 4 **ounces cream cheese, softened**
- ½ **cup canned pumpkin**
- 1 **egg**
- 3 **tablespoons sugar**
- ¾ **teaspoon pumpkin pie spice**
- **Pinch salt**

BROWNIES

- ½ **cup (1 stick) unsalted butter**
- 6 **ounces semisweet chocolate, chopped**
- 1 **cup sugar**
- 3 **eggs**
- 1 **teaspoon vanilla**
- ¾ **cup all-purpose flour**
- 2 **tablespoons unsweetened cocoa powder**
- ½ **teaspoon salt**

1. Preheat oven to 350°F. Spray 8-inch square baking pan with nonstick cooking spray or line with parchment paper.

2. For swirl, combine cream cheese, pumpkin, 1 egg, 3 tablespoons sugar, pumpkin pie spice and pinch of salt in medium bowl; whisk until smooth.

3. For brownies, melt butter and chocolate in medium saucepan over low heat, stirring frequently. Remove from heat; stir in 1 cup sugar until blended. Beat in 3 eggs, one at a time, until well blended. Stir in vanilla. Add flour, cocoa and ½ teaspoon salt; stir until blended. Reserve ⅓ cup brownie batter in small bowl; spread remaining batter in prepared pan.

4. Spread swirl mixture evenly over brownie batter. Drop reserved brownie batter by teaspoonfuls over pumpkin layer; draw tip of knife through top of both batters to marbleize. (If reserved brownie batter has become very thick upon standing, microwave on LOW (30%) 20 to 30 seconds or until loosened, stirring at 10-second intervals.)

5. Bake 28 to 30 minutes or just until center is set and edges begin to pull away from sides of pan. (Toothpick will come out with fudgy crumbs.) Cool completely in pan on wire rack.

HAWAIIAN BARS

Makes 16 to 20 bars

1⅓ cups all-purpose flour

1 teaspoon baking powder

¼ teaspoon baking soda

½ teaspoon salt

10 tablespoons unsalted butter, cubed

1 cup packed dark brown sugar

⅓ cup granulated sugar

1 teaspoon vanilla

2 eggs

¾ cup coarsely chopped salted macadamia nuts

¾ cup sweetened shredded coconut

1. Preheat oven to 350°F. Line 9-inch square baking pan with parchment paper or spray with nonstick cooking spray. Whisk flour, baking powder, baking soda and salt in medium bowl.

2. Melt butter in large heavy saucepan over low heat. Remove from heat; whisk in sugars and vanilla. Whisk in eggs one at a time. Add flour mixture, nuts and coconut; mix well. Spread batter in prepared pan.

3. Bake 30 minutes or until edges begin to pull away from sides of pan. Cool completely in pan on wire rack. Cut into bars.

NOTE

These bars firm up and taste better the day after they are made.

PUMPKIN CHEESECAKE BARS

Makes about 2 dozen bars

1½ **cups gingersnap crumbs,
plus additional for garnish**

6 **tablespoons (¾ stick)
unsalted butter, melted**

2 **eggs**

¼ **cup plus 2 tablespoons
sugar, divided**

2½ **teaspoons vanilla, divided**

12 **ounces cream cheese,
softened**

1¼ **cups canned pumpkin**

1 **teaspoon ground cinnamon**

¼ **teaspoon ground ginger**

¼ **teaspoon ground nutmeg**

¼ **teaspoon ground cloves**

1 **cup sour cream**

1. Preheat oven to 325°F. Line 13×9-inch baking pan with parchment paper or spray with nonstick cooking spray.

2. Combine 1½ cups gingersnap crumbs and butter in small bowl; mix well. Press into prepared pan. Bake 10 minutes.

3. Meanwhile, combine eggs, ¼ cup sugar and 1½ teaspoons vanilla in food processor or blender; process 1 minute or until smooth. Add cream cheese and pumpkin; process until well blended. Stir in cinnamon, ginger, nutmeg and cloves. Pour evenly over hot crust.

4. Bake 40 minutes. Whisk sour cream, remaining 2 tablespoons sugar and 1 teaspoon vanilla in small bowl until blended. Remove cheesecake from oven; spread sour cream mixture evenly over top. Bake 5 minutes. Turn off oven; open door halfway and let cheesecake cool completely in oven. Refrigerate at least 2 hours before serving. Garnish with additional gingersnap crumbs.

WHITE CHOCOLATE
TOFFEE ALMOND BARS

Makes 2 to 3 dozen bars

1 cup (2 sticks) butter, softened

1 cup sugar

1 egg

2 tablespoons instant espresso powder or instant coffee granules

1 teaspoon almond extract

2¼ cups all-purpose flour

⅔ cup sliced almonds, toasted*

⅔ cup white chocolate chips

⅓ cup toffee bits

*To toast almonds, spread on baking sheet. Bake in preheated 350°F oven 5 to 7 minutes or until lightly browned and fragrant, stirring frequently.

1. Preheat oven to 350°F. Line 13×9-inch baking pan with parchment paper or spray with nonstick cooking spray.

2. Beat butter and sugar in large bowl with electric mixer at medium-high speed about 3 minutes or until light and fluffy. Add egg, espresso powder and almond extract; beat until well blended. Gradually beat in flour at low speed just until blended. Stir in almonds, white chocolate chips and toffee bits. Spread dough evenly in prepared pan.

3. Bake 23 to 28 minutes or until center is set and edges are lightly browned. Cool completely in pan on wire rack. Cut into bars.

⋝ CHOCOLATE PECAN BARS ⋜

Makes 2 to 3 dozen bars

CRUST

- **1⅓ cups all-purpose flour**
- **½ cup (1 stick) unsalted butter, softened**
- **¼ cup packed brown sugar**
- **½ teaspoon salt**

TOPPING

- **3 eggs, lightly beaten**
- **¾ cup light corn syrup**
- **2 tablespoons unsalted butter, melted and cooled**
- **½ teaspoon vanilla**
- **½ teaspoon almond extract**
- **¾ cup milk chocolate chips**
- **¾ cup semisweet chocolate chips**
- **¾ cup chopped pecans, toasted***
- **¾ cup granulated sugar**

*To toast pecans, spread on baking sheet. Bake in preheated 350°F oven 5 to 7 minutes or until lightly browned and fragrant, stirring frequently.

1. Preheat oven to 350°F. Line 13×9-inch baking pan with parchment paper or spray with nonstick cooking spray.

2. For crust, combine flour, ½ cup butter, brown sugar and salt in medium bowl; mix with fork until crumbly. Press into prepared baking pan. Bake 12 to 15 minutes or until lightly browned. Let stand 10 minutes.

3. Meanwhile for topping, whisk eggs in large bowl with fork until lightly beaten. Add corn syrup, 2 tablespoons butter, vanilla and almond extract; stir with fork until well blended (do not beat). Fold in chocolate chips, pecans and granulated sugar until blended. Pour over baked crust.

4. Bake 25 to 30 minutes or until toothpick inserted into center comes out clean. Cool completely in pan on wire rack. Store in refrigerator in airtight container.

⋝ NOTE ⋜

To easily remove corn syrup from a measuring cup, spray the inside first before measuring.

CHOCOLATE CHIP SHORTBREAD

Makes about 1 dozen bars

½ **cup (1 stick) unsalted butter, softened**

½ **cup sugar**

2 **tablespoons packed brown sugar**

1 **teaspoon vanilla**

1 **cup all-purpose flour**

½ **teaspoon salt**

½ **cup plus 2 tablespoons mini semisweet chocolate chips, divided**

1. Preheat oven to 350°F.

2. Beat butter and sugars in large bowl with electric mixer at medium speed until light and fluffy. Beat in vanilla. Add flour and salt; beat at low speed until combined. Stir in ½ cup chocolate chips. Press dough into 8- or 9-inch square baking pan. Sprinkle with remaining 2 tablespoons chocolate chips; press lightly into dough.

3. Bake 15 to 17 minutes or until edges are golden brown. Cool completely in pan on wire rack. Cut into rectangles.

VARIATION

For wedges, press dough into two 8-inch round baking pans. Bake 12 to 15 minutes or until edges are golden brown and centers are set. Cool completely in pan on wire rack; cut each into 8 wedges.

BROWN SUGAR DREAM BARS

Makes about 4 dozen bars

1½ **cups packed brown sugar, divided**

½ **cup (1 stick) unsalted butter, softened**

1 **egg yolk**

1 **cup plus 2 tablespoons all-purpose flour, divided**

½ **teaspoon salt**

2 **eggs**

1 **cup semisweet chocolate chips**

½ **cup chopped toasted walnuts***

To toast walnuts, spread in single layer on baking sheet. Bake in preheated 350°F oven 5 to 7 minutes or until golden brown, stirring frequently.

1. Preheat oven to 375°F. Grease 13×9-inch baking pan or line with parchment paper.

2. Beat ½ cup brown sugar, butter and egg yolk in large bowl with electric mixer at medium speed until light and smooth. Add 1 cup flour and salt; mix on low speed until well blended. Press dough into prepared pan. Bake 12 to 15 minutes or until golden.

3. Meanwhile, beat remaining 1 cup brown sugar, 2 tablespoons flour and whole eggs in same bowl with electric mixer at medium-high speed until light and frothy. Spread mixture over partially baked crust.

4. Return to oven; bake about 15 minutes or until topping is set. Immediately sprinkle with chocolate chips. Let stand until chips melt, then spread chocolate evenly over bars. Sprinkle with walnuts. Cool completely in pan on wire rack. Cut into bars.

VIENNESE MERINGUE BARS

Makes 2 to 3 dozen bars

1 cup (2 sticks) unsalted butter, softened

1¼ cups sugar, divided

2 egg yolks

½ teaspoon salt

2¼ cups all-purpose flour

1 cup seedless raspberry jam, stirred

1½ cups mini semisweet chocolate chips

3 egg whites

½ cup slivered almonds, toasted

Fresh raspberries (optional)

1. Preheat oven to 350°F. Line 15×10-inch sheet pan with parchment paper or leave ungreased.

2. Beat butter and ½ cup sugar in large bowl with electric mixer at medium speed 3 to 4 minutes until light and fluffy. Beat in egg yolks and salt. Gradually add flour. Beat at low speed until well blended. With buttered fingers, pat dough evenly into prepared pan.

3. Bake 22 to 25 minutes or until light golden brown. Remove from oven; immediately spread jam over crust. Sprinkle evenly with chocolate chips.

4. For meringue topping, beat egg whites in clean large bowl with electric mixer at high speed until foamy. Gradually beat in remaining ¾ cup sugar until stiff peaks form. Gently stir in almonds with rubber spatula.

5. Spread meringue evenly over chocolate mixture; spread evenly with small spatula. Bake 20 to 25 minutes or until golden brown. Cool completely on wire rack. Cut into bars; garnish with raspberries.

PUMPKIN STREUSEL BARS

Makes 2 to 3 dozen bars

1½ **cups all-purpose flour, divided**

½ **cup packed brown sugar**

¼ **cup (½ stick) unsalted butter, cut into small pieces**

1 **cup coarsely chopped pecans**

1½ **teaspoons baking powder**

1 **teaspoon ground cinnamon**

½ **teaspoon salt**

¼ **teaspoon baking soda**

⅛ **teaspoon ground ginger**

1 **cup granulated sugar**

1 **cup canned pumpkin**

½ **cup vegetable oil**

2 **eggs**

2 **tablespoons unsalted butter, melted**

1. Preheat oven to 350°F. Spray 13×9-inch baking pan with nonstick cooking spray or line with foil.

2. For streusel, combine ½ cup flour and brown sugar in medium bowl. Cut in ¼ cup butter with pastry blender or fingers until mixture resembles coarse crumbs. Stir in pecans.

3. Combine remaining 1 cup flour, baking powder, cinnamon, salt, baking soda and ginger in medium bowl; mix well. Beat granulated sugar, pumpkin, oil, eggs and melted butter in large bowl with electric mixer at medium speed until well blended. Gradually beat in flour mixture at low speed just until blended. Spread batter in prepared pan; sprinkle with streusel.

4. Bake 35 minutes or until toothpick inserted into center comes out clean. Cool completely in pan on wire rack. Cut into squares.

CARAMEL CHOCOLATE CHUNK BLONDIES

Makes 2 to 3 dozen blondies

- 1½ **cups all-purpose flour**
- 1 **teaspoon baking powder**
- 1 **teaspoon salt**
- ¾ **cup granulated sugar**
- ¾ **cup packed brown sugar**
- ½ **cup (1 stick) unsalted butter, softened**
- 2 **eggs**
- 1½ **teaspoons vanilla**
- 1 **package (11½ ounces) semisweet chocolate chunks *or* 10 ounces chopped bittersweet chocolate**
- 5 **tablespoons caramel ice cream topping**
- **Flaky sea salt (optional)**

1. Preheat oven to 350°F. Line 13×9-inch baking pan with parchment paper or spray with nonstick cooking spray. Whisk flour, baking powder and 1 teaspoon salt in medium bowl.

2. Beat sugars and butter in large bowl with electric mixer at medium speed 2 minutes or until smooth and creamy. Beat in eggs and vanilla until well blended. Add flour mixture; beat at low speed until blended. Stir in chocolate chunks.

3. Spread batter evenly in prepared pan. Drop spoonfuls of caramel topping over batter; swirl into batter with knife. Sprinkle with sea salt, if desired.

4. Bake about 30 minutes or until edges are golden brown (center will be puffed and will not look set). Cool completely in pan on wire rack. Remove from pan using parchment; cut into bars.

⇒ CELEBRATION BROWNIES ⇐

Makes 2 to 3 dozen brownies

1 cup (2 sticks) butter

8 ounces semisweet baking chocolate, coarsely chopped

1 cup sugar

4 eggs

1 teaspoon vanilla

1 teaspoon salt

1¼ cups all-purpose flour

2 cups dark or semisweet chocolate chips, divided

¼ cup whipping cream

1 container (about 2 ounces) rainbow nonpareils

1. Preheat oven to 350°F. Spray 13×9-inch baking pan with nonstick cooking spray or line with parchment paper.

2. Heat butter and chocolate in large heavy saucepan over low heat; stir until melted and smooth. Remove from heat; stir in sugar until blended. Stir in eggs, one at a time, until well blended after each addition. Stir in vanilla and salt. Add flour and 1 cup chocolate chips; stir just until blended. Spread batter evenly in prepared pan.

3. Bake 22 to 25 minutes or until center is set and toothpick inserted into center comes out clean. Cool completely in pan on wire rack.

4. For topping, heat cream in small saucepan over medium-low heat until bubbles appear around edge of pan. Remove from heat; add remaining 1 cup chocolate chips. Let stand 1 minute; whisk until smooth and well blended. Spread evenly over brownies; top with nonpareils.

BAKLAVA

Makes about 32 pieces

4 cups walnuts, shelled pistachio nuts and/or slivered almonds (1 pound)

1¼ cups sugar, divided

2 teaspoons ground cinnamon

¼ teaspoon ground cloves

1 cup (2 sticks) unsalted butter, melted

1 package (16 ounces) frozen phyllo dough (about 20 sheets), thawed

1½ cups water

¾ cup honey

2 (2-inch-long) strips lemon peel

1 tablespoon fresh lemon juice

1 cinnamon stick

3 whole cloves

1. Place half of walnuts in food processor. Pulse until nuts are finely chopped but not pasty. Transfer to large bowl; repeat with remaining nuts. Add ½ cup sugar, ground cinnamon and ground cloves to nuts; mix well.

2. Preheat oven to 325°F. Brush 13×9-inch baking dish with some of melted butter or line with foil, leaving overhang on two sides for easy removal. Unroll phyllo dough and place on large sheet of waxed paper. Trim phyllo sheets to 13×9 inches. Cover phyllo with plastic wrap and damp, clean kitchen towel to prevent drying out.

3. Place 1 phyllo sheet in bottom of dish, folding in edges if too long; brush with butter. Repeat with 7 additional phyllo sheets, brushing each sheet with butter as it is layered. Sprinkle about ½ cup nut mixture evenly over layered phyllo. Top nuts with 3 additional layers of phyllo, brushing each sheet with butter. Sprinkle with ½ cup nut mixture. Repeat layering and brushing of 3 phyllo sheets with ½ cup nut mixture two more times. Top final layer of nut mixture with remaining phyllo sheets, brushing each sheet with butter.

4. Score baklava lengthwise into 4 equal sections, then cut diagonally at 1½-inch intervals to form diamond shapes. Sprinkle top lightly with water to prevent top phyllo layers from curling up during baking. Bake 50 to 60 minutes or until golden brown.

5. Meanwhile, combine 1½ cups water, remaining ¾ cup sugar, honey, lemon peel, lemon juice, cinnamon stick and whole cloves in medium saucepan; bring to a boil over high heat. Reduce heat to low; simmer 15 minutes. Strain hot syrup; drizzle evenly over hot baklava. Cool completely in pan on wire rack. Cut into pieces along score lines.

SEVEN-LAYER DESSERT

Makes 2 to 3 dozen bars

½ cup (1 stick) unsalted butter, melted

1 teaspoon vanilla

1 cup graham cracker crumbs

1 cup butterscotch chips

1 cup chocolate chips

1 cup shredded coconut

1 cup chopped nuts

1 can (14 ounces) sweetened condensed milk

1. Preheat oven to 350°F.

2. Pour butter into 13×9-inch baking pan. Add vanilla. Sprinkle cracker crumbs over butter. Layer butterscotch chips over crumbs, followed by chocolate chips, coconut and nuts. Pour condensed milk over mixture.

3. Bake 25 minutes or until lightly browned. Cool completely in pan on wire rack. Cut into bars.

SANDWICH COOKIES

CHOCOLATE HAZELNUT SANDWICH COOKIES

Makes 30 sandwich cookies

- ¾ **cup (1½ sticks) unsalted butter, slightly softened**
- ¾ **cup sugar**
- 3 **egg yolks**
- 1 **teaspoon vanilla**
- 2 **cups all-purpose flour**
- ¼ **teaspoon salt**
- ⅔ **cup chocolate hazelnut spread**

1. Beat butter and sugar in large bowl with electric mixer at medium speed 1 minute. Beat in egg yolks and vanilla until well blended. Add flour and salt; beat just until combined. Divide dough in half. Shape each piece into 6×1½-inch log. Wrap in plastic wrap; refrigerate at least 2 hours or until firm.

2. Preheat oven to 350°F. Line cookie sheets with parchment paper. Cut dough into ⅛-inch-thick slices; place 1 inch apart on prepared cookie sheets.

3. Bake about 10 minutes or until edges are light brown. Cool on cookie sheets 5 minutes. Remove to wire racks; cool completely.

4. Spread 1 teaspoon hazelnut spread on flat side of half of cookies; top with remaining cookies. Store covered in airtight container.

MARSHMALLOW SANDWICH COOKIES

Makes about 2 dozen sandwich cookies

- **2 cups all-purpose flour**
- **½ cup unsweetened cocoa powder**
- **2 teaspoons baking soda**
- **½ teaspoon salt**
- **1½ cups sugar, divided**
- **10 tablespoons unsalted butter, softened**
- **¼ cup light corn syrup**
- **1 egg**
- **1 teaspoon vanilla**
- **24 large marshmallows**

1. Preheat oven to 350°F. Whisk flour, cocoa, baking soda and salt in medium bowl.

2. Beat 1¼ cups sugar and butter in large bowl with electric mixer at medium-high speed 3 to 4 minutes or until light and fluffy. Beat in corn syrup, egg and vanilla until blended. Gradually beat in flour mixture at low speed just until blended. Cover and refrigerate 15 minutes or until dough is firm enough to shape into balls.

3. Place remaining ¼ cup sugar in small bowl. Shape dough into 1-inch balls; roll in sugar to coat. Place cookies 3 inches apart on ungreased cookie sheets.

4. Bake 10 to 11 minutes or until set. Cool on cookie sheets 3 minutes. Remove to wire racks; cool completely.

5. Place one cookie on microwavable plate. Top with one marshmallow. Microwave on HIGH about 10 seconds or until marshmallow is softened. Immediately place another cookie, flat side down, on top of hot marshmallow; press together. Repeat with remaining cookies and marshmallows.

MINI LEMON SANDWICH COOKIES

Makes 4½ dozen sandwich cookies

2 cups all-purpose flour

1¼ cups (2½ sticks) unsalted butter, softened, divided

½ cup granulated sugar, divided

⅓ cup whipping cream

1 teaspoon grated lemon peel

⅛ teaspoon lemon extract

¾ cup powdered sugar

2 to 3 teaspoons lemon juice

1 teaspoon vanilla

Yellow food coloring (optional)

1. For cookies, beat flour, 1 cup butter, ¼ cup granulated sugar, cream, lemon peel and lemon extract in large bowl with electric mixer at medium speed 2 to 3 minutes or until well blended. Divide dough into thirds. Wrap each piece in waxed paper; refrigerate until firm.

2. Preheat oven to 375°F. Place remaining ¼ cup granulated sugar in shallow bowl. Roll out each piece of dough to ⅛-inch thickness on well-floured surface. Cut out dough with 1½-inch round cookie cutter. Dip both sides of each cookie in sugar. Place 1 inch apart on ungreased cookie sheets; pierce several times with fork.

3. Bake 6 to 9 minutes or until cookies are slightly puffed but not brown. Cool on cookie sheets 1 minute. Remove to wire racks; cool completely.

4. For filling, beat powdered sugar, remaining ¼ cup butter, lemon juice and vanilla in large bowl with electric mixer at medium speed 1 to 2 minutes or until smooth. Tint with food coloring, if desired. Spread ½ teaspoon filling each on flat side of half of cookies; top with remaining cookies.

BLACK AND WHITE SANDWICH COOKIES

Makes 22 to 24 cookies

COOKIES

- 1¼ cups (2½ sticks) unsalted butter
- ¾ cup superfine or granulated sugar
- 1 egg
- 1½ teaspoons vanilla
- 2⅓ cups all-purpose flour, divided
- ¼ teaspoon salt
- ⅓ cup unsweetened cocoa powder

FILLING

- ½ cup (1 stick) unsalted butter
- 4 ounces cream cheese, softened
- 2 cups plus 2 tablespoons powdered sugar
- 2 tablespoons unsweetened cocoa powder

1. For cookies, beat 1¼ cups butter and superfine sugar in large bowl with electric mixer until creamy. Beat in egg and vanilla until well blended. Beat in 2 cups flour and salt at low speed just until combined.

2. Remove half of dough to medium bowl; stir in remaining ⅓ cup flour. Add ⅓ cup cocoa to dough in mixer bowl; beat just until blended. Wrap doughs separately in plastic wrap; refrigerate 30 minutes or until firm.

3. Preheat oven to 350°F. Line cookie sheets with parchment paper or leave ungreased. Roll out plain dough on floured surface to ¼-inch thickness. Cut out 2-inch circles with round cookie cutter; place 2 inches apart on prepared cookie sheets. Repeat with chocolate dough.

4. Bake 8 to 10 minutes. Remove to wire racks; cool completely.

5. For filling, beat ½ cup butter and cream cheese in medium bowl with electric mixer until well blended. Add 2 cups powdered sugar; beat until creamy. Remove half of filling to small bowl; stir in remaining 2 tablespoons powdered sugar. Add 2 tablespoons cocoa to filling in mixer bowl; beat until smooth.

6. Pipe or spread chocolate frosting on flat side of half of plain cookies; top with remaining plain cookies. Pipe or spread vanilla frosting on flat side of half of chocolate cookies; top with remaining chocolate cookies.

PB & J SANDWICH COOKIES

Makes about 2½ dozen cookies

COOKIES

- 1 cup (2 sticks) unsalted butter, softened
- ½ cup powdered sugar
- 2 tablespoons packed brown sugar
- ¼ teaspoon salt
- 2 cups all-purpose flour
- 2 tablespoons creamy peanut butter
- 2 tablespoons strawberry jam
- 3 to 4 drops red food color

PEANUT BUTTER FILLING

- ⅓ cup creamy peanut butter
- 2 tablespoons unsalted butter, softened
- 1 cup powdered sugar
- 3 tablespoons milk or half-and-half

1. Beat butter, powdered sugar, brown sugar and salt in large bowl with electric mixer at medium speed 3 to 4 minutes or until light and fluffy. Add flour, ½ cup at a time, beating well after each addition. Divide dough in half; set one half aside. Add 2 tablespoons peanut butter to remaining dough in bowl; beat until blended. Shape peanut butter dough into 10-inch log; wrap in plastic wrap and chill 1 hour.

2. Add jam and food coloring to reserved dough; beat until blended. Shape strawberry dough into 10-inch log. Wrap in plastic wrap; refrigerate 1 hour.

3. Preheat oven to 300°F. Cut each log into ⅛-inch-thick slices; place on ungreased cookie sheets. Bake 15 to 18 minutes or until cookies are set and lightly browned. Cool on cookie sheets 5 minutes. Remove to wire racks; cool completely.

4. For filling, beat ⅓ cup peanut butter and 2 tablespoons butter in large bowl with electric mixer at medium speed until smooth. Gradually add 1 cup powdered sugar; blend well. Add milk; beat until light and fluffy. Spread about 1½ teaspoons filling over flat sides of peanut butter cookies; top with strawberry cookies.

CHOCOLATE CHIP SANDWICH COOKIES

Makes 16 sandwich cookies

¾ cup plus ⅓ cup packed brown sugar

½ cup (1 stick) unsalted butter, softened

1 egg

1 teaspoon vanilla

¾ teaspoon baking soda

½ teaspoon salt

1¾ cups all-purpose flour

3 cups semisweet chocolate chips, divided

6 tablespoons whipping cream

1. Preheat oven to 350°F. Line cookie sheets with parchment paper.

2. Beat brown sugar and butter in large bowl with electric mixer at medium speed 5 minutes or until light and fluffy. Add egg and vanilla; beat until well blended. Beat in baking soda and salt. Gradually beat in flour at low speed just until blended. Stir in 1½ cups chocolate chips. Drop heaping tablespoonfuls of dough 2 inches apart onto prepared cookie sheets.

3. Bake about 10 minutes or until cookies are just beginning to brown around edges but are still very soft in center. (Cookies will look underbaked.) Cool on cookie sheets 5 minutes. Remove to wire racks; cool completely.

4. For filling, bring cream to a simmer in small saucepan over medium-low heat. Add remaining 1½ cups chocolate chips to cream; let stand 1 minute. Stir until smooth. Refrigerate 1 hour, stirring occasionally. (Filling should be thick enough to spread and still be shiny when stirred.)

5. Spread heaping tablespoonful of chocolate filling onto bottoms of half of cookies. Top with remaining cookies.

CARDAMOM CHOCOLATE SANDWICHES

Makes about 1 dozen sandwich cookies

1½ cups all-purpose flour

1 teaspoon ground cardamom

½ teaspoon baking soda

½ teaspoon salt

1¼ cups (2½ sticks) unsalted butter, softened, divided

¾ cup packed dark brown sugar

1 egg

Pearl sugar or sparkling sugar

1 cup dark chocolate chips *or* 4 ounces bittersweet chocolate, chopped

2 cups powdered sugar

2 tablespoons whipping cream or milk

1. Whisk flour, cardamom, baking soda and salt in medium bowl. Beat ¾ cup butter and brown sugar in large bowl with electric mixer at medium speed until light and fluffy. Beat in egg. Add flour mixture; beat on low speed just until blended. Shape dough into a disc; wrap with plastic wrap. Refrigerate 1 hour or until firm. (Dough may be kept refrigerated up to 3 days.)

2. Preheat oven to 300°F. Line cookie sheets with parchment paper. Roll out dough on well floured surface ⅛ inch thick. Cut out 2-inch circles with cookie cutter; place on prepared cookie sheets. Sprinkle half of cookies with pearl sugar. Bake 7 to 8 minutes or until cookies are set and lightly browned around edges. Cool on cookie sheets 2 minutes. Remove to wire racks; cool completely.

3. For filling, heat chocolate in medium microwavable bowl on HIGH 1½ minutes or until melted, stirring after 1 minute. Beat remaining ½ cup butter and powdered sugar in large bowl with electric mixer at medium-low speed about 1 minute or until creamy. Beat at medium speed until fluffy. Add melted chocolate and cream; beat at medium-high speed about 1 minute or until well blended and fluffy. Spread filling on flat side of one plain cookie; top with decorated cookie. Repeat with remaining cookies and filling.

MINI CHOCOLATE WHOOPIE PIES

Makes about 2 dozen sandwiches

1¾ cups all-purpose flour

½ cup unsweetened Dutch process or natural cocoa powder

¾ teaspoon baking powder

½ teaspoon baking soda

½ teaspoon salt

1 cup packed brown sugar

1 cup (2 sticks) unsalted butter, softened, divided

1 egg

1½ teaspoons vanilla, divided

1 cup milk

1 cup marshmallow creme

1 cup powdered sugar

1. Preheat oven to 350°F. Line cookie sheets with parchment paper. Whisk flour, cocoa, baking powder, baking soda and salt in medium bowl.

2. Beat brown sugar and ½ cup butter in large bowl with electric mixer at medium-high speed 3 to 4 minutes or until light and fluffy. Beat in egg and 1 teaspoon vanilla until well blended. Alternately add flour mixture and milk, beating at low speed after each addition until smooth and well blended. Drop dough by heaping teaspoonfuls 2 inches apart onto prepared cookie sheets.

3. Bake 8 to 10 minutes or until cookies are puffed and tops spring back when lightly touched. Cool on cookie sheets 10 minutes. Remove to wire racks; cool completely.

4. Meanwhile for filling, beat remaining ½ cup butter, ½ teaspoon vanilla, marshmallow creme and powdered sugar in large bowl with electric mixer at high speed 2 minutes or until light and fluffy.

5. Pipe or spread heaping teaspoon filling onto flat side of half of cookies; top with remaining cookies.

TINY PEANUT BUTTER SANDWICHES

Makes 6 to 7 dozen sandwiches

1¼ cups all-purpose flour

½ teaspoon baking powder

½ teaspoon baking soda

¼ teaspoon salt

½ cup (1 stick) unsalted butter, softened

½ cup granulated sugar

½ cup packed brown sugar

½ cup creamy peanut butter

1 egg

1 teaspoon vanilla

½ cup whipping cream

1 cup semisweet chocolate chips

1. Preheat oven to 350°F. Whisk flour, baking powder, baking soda and salt in medium bowl.

2. Beat butter and sugars in large bowl with electric mixer at medium speed until light and fluffy. Beat in peanut butter, egg and vanilla until well blended. Gradually beat in flour mixture at low speed until blended.

3. Shape dough by ½ teaspoonfuls into balls; place 1 inch apart on ungreased cookie sheets. Flatten balls slightly in crisscross pattern with fork.

4. Bake 6 minutes or just until set. Cool on cookie sheets 4 minutes. Remove to wire racks; cool completely.

5. For filling, bring cream to a simmer in small saucepan over low heat. Add chocolate chips; stir until smooth. Let stand 10 minutes or until filling thickens to desired consistency.

6. Spread scant teaspoon filling on flat side of half of cookies; top with remaining cookies.

CHOCOLATE CHIP S'MORE BITES

Makes about 4 dozen s'mores

2 cups all-purpose flour

1 teaspoon baking soda

½ teaspoon salt

¾ cup (1½ sticks) unsalted butter, softened

¾ cup packed brown sugar

½ cup granulated sugar

1 egg

1¼ teaspoons vanilla

2 cups semisweet chocolate chips, divided

¼ cup plus 2 tablespoons whipping cream

½ cup marshmallow creme

½ cup sour cream

1. Preheat oven to 325°F. Spray 13×9-inch baking pan with nonstick cooking spray. Whisk flour, baking soda and ½ teaspoon salt in medium bowl.

2. Beat butter and sugars in large bowl with electric mixer at medium-high speed until light and fluffy. Add egg and vanilla; beat until blended. Add flour mixture; beat on low speed until blended. Stir in 1¼ cups chocolate chips. Bake 20 minutes or until light golden brown and just set. Cool completely in pan on wire rack.

3. Bring cream to a simmer in small saucepan over low heat. Add remaining ¾ cup chocolate chips; stir until smooth. Let stand 10 minutes or until mixture thickens.

4. Combine marshmallow creme and sour cream in small bowl until smooth.

5. Cut bars into 1¼-inch squares with sharp knife. For each s'more, spread scant teaspoon chocolate mixture on bottom of one square; spread scant teaspoon marshmallow mixture on bottom of second square. Press together to form s'mores.

MINT CHOCOLATE DELIGHTS

Makes 2 dozen sandwich cookies

1½ **cups all-purpose flour**

¼ **cup unsweetened cocoa powder**

½ **teaspoon salt, divided**

1 **cup (2 sticks) unsalted butter, softened, divided**

½ **cup granulated sugar**

⅓ **cup packed dark brown sugar**

⅓ **cup semisweet chocolate chips, melted and slightly cooled**

1 **egg**

½ **teaspoon vanilla**

2½ **cups powdered sugar**

½ **teaspoon mint extract**

3 **to 4 drops red food coloring**

2 **to 3 tablespoons milk or half-and-half**

1. Combine flour, cocoa and ¼ teaspoon salt in small bowl. Beat ½ cup butter, granulated sugar and brown sugar in large bowl with electric mixer at medium speed until creamy. Add melted chocolate, egg and vanilla; beat until well blended. Gradually beat in flour mixture at low speed just until blended. Shape dough into 16-inch log. Wrap in plastic wrap; refrigerate 1 hour or until firm.

2. Preheat oven to 350°F. Lightly grease cookie sheets. Cut log into ⅛-inch slices. Place 2 inches apart on prepared cookie sheets.

3. Bake 10 minutes or until set. Cool on cookie sheets 5 minutes. Remove to wire racks; cool completely.

4. For filling, beat powdered sugar, remaining ½ cup butter and ¼ teaspoon salt in large bowl with electric mixer at medium speed until well blended. Add mint extract and food coloring; beat until well blended and evenly tinted. Beat in milk, 1 tablespoon at a time, until fluffy. Pipe or spread filling on flat side of one cookie; top with second cookie. Repeat with remaining filling and cookies.

LINZER SANDWICH COOKIES

Makes about 2 dozen sandwich cookies

1⅔ **cups all-purpose flour**

¼ **teaspoon baking powder**

¼ **teaspoon salt**

¾ **cup granulated sugar**

½ **cup (1 stick) unsalted butter, softened**

1 **egg**

1 **teaspoon vanilla**

Powdered sugar (optional)

Seedless red raspberry jam

1. Combine flour, baking powder and salt in medium bowl. Beat granulated sugar and butter in large bowl with electric mixer at medium speed until light and fluffy. Beat in egg and vanilla until blended. Gradually beat in flour mixture at low speed just until blended. Divide dough in half. Wrap each half in plastic wrap; refrigerate 2 hours or until firm.

2. Preheat oven to 375°F. Roll out half of dough on lightly floured surface to ¼-inch thickness. Cut out circles with 1½-inch floured scalloped or plain round cookie cutters. (If dough becomes too soft, refrigerate several minutes before continuing.) Place cutouts 2 inches apart on ungreased cookie sheets.

3. Roll out remaining half of dough and cut out circles. Cut 1-inch centers of different shapes from circles. Place 2 inches apart on ungreased cookie sheets.

4. Bake 7 to 9 minutes or until edges are lightly browned. Cool on cookie sheets 2 minutes. Remove to wire racks; cool completely.

5. Sprinkle powdered sugar over cookies with holes, if desired. Spread jam on flat sides of whole cookies; top with sugar-dusted cookies.

FRUIT FLAVORS

LEMON SQUARES

Makes 2 to 3 dozen squares

CRUST

- **1 cup (2 sticks) unsalted butter, softened**
- **½ cup granulated sugar**
- **½ teaspoon salt**
- **2 cups all-purpose flour**

FILLING

- **3 cups granulated sugar**
- **1 cup all-purpose flour**
- **4 eggs plus 2 egg yolks, at room temperature**
- **⅔ cup fresh lemon juice**
- **2 tablespoons grated lemon peel**
- **½ teaspoon baking powder**
- **Powdered sugar**

1. Beat butter, ½ cup granulated sugar and salt in large bowl with electric mixer at medium speed until light and fluffy. Gradually beat in 2 cups flour at low speed just until blended.

2. Press dough into 13×9-inch baking pan, building edges up ½ inch on all sides. Refrigerate at least 20 minutes.

3. Preheat oven to 350°F. Bake 15 to 20 minutes or until very lightly browned. Cool on wire rack.

4. Whisk 3 cups granulated sugar, 1 cup flour, eggs and egg yolks, lemon juice, lemon peel and baking powder in large bowl until well blended. Pour over crust.

5. Bake 30 to 35 minutes until filling is set. Cool completely in pan on wire rack. Cut into squares; sprinkle with powdered sugar.

TANGY LEMON RASPBERRY BARS

Makes 12 to 16 bars

¾ cup packed brown sugar

½ cup (1 stick) unsalted butter, softened

Grated peel of 1 lemon

1 cup all-purpose flour

1 cup old-fashioned oats

1 teaspoon baking powder

½ teaspoon salt

½ cup raspberry jam

1. Preheat oven to 350°F. Spray 8-inch square baking pan with nonstick cooking spray.

2. Beat brown sugar, butter and lemon peel in large bowl with electric mixer at medium speed until combined. Add flour, oats, baking powder and salt; beat at low speed until combined. Reserve ¼ cup mixture. Press remaining mixture into prepared pan. Spread jam over top; sprinkle with reserved mixture.

3. Bake 25 minutes or until edges are lightly brown. Cool completely in pan on wire rack. Cut into bars.

CRANBERRY-LIME DESSERT SQUARES

Makes 2 to 3 dozen squares

2 cups all-purpose flour

½ cup powdered sugar, plus additional for dusting

1 tablespoon plus 1 teaspoon grated lime peel

¼ teaspoon plus ⅛ teaspoon salt

1 cup (2 sticks) unsalted butter

2 cups granulated sugar

4 eggs

¼ cup cornstarch

¼ cup fresh lime juice (about 2 limes)

1 teaspoon baking powder

1 cup dried cranberries

1. Preheat oven to 350°F. Line 13×9-inch baking pan with parchment paper.

2. Combine flour, ½ cup powdered sugar, 1 tablespoon lime peel and ¼ teaspoon salt in medium bowl. Cut in butter with pastry blender or electric mixer on low speed until mixture forms coarse crumbs. Press mixture evenly into prepared baking pan. Bake 18 to 20 minutes or until golden brown.

3. Combine granulated sugar and eggs in large bowl. Attach whisk attachment to stand mixer. Beat egg mixture on high speed 5 to 6 minutes or until thick, pale and triple in volume. Add cornstarch, lime juice, remaining 1 teaspoon lime peel, baking powder and remaining ⅛ teaspoon salt; beat 3 to 5 minutes or until very well blended. Stir in cranberries. Pour over warm crust.

4. Bake about 25 minutes until golden brown and set. Cool completely on wire rack. Sprinkle with additional powdered sugar. Refrigerate at least 2 hours. Cut into squares; serve cold. Store leftovers in refrigerator.

APRICOT-GLAZED SQUARES

Makes 16 squares

¾ cup plus 2 tablespoons all-purpose flour

½ teaspoon baking soda

1 teaspoon ground cinnamon

¼ teaspoon salt

¼ cup sugar

¼ cup (½ stick) unsalted butter, softened

¼ cup maple syrup

1 egg

⅓ cup buttermilk*

1 teaspoon vanilla

¼ cup apricot jam

*Or substitute 1 teaspoon vinegar stirred into ⅓ cup milk.

1. Preheat oven to 350°F. Lightly grease 9-inch square baking pan. Whisk flour, baking soda, cinnamon and salt in small bowl.

2. Beat sugar and butter in medium bowl with electric mixer at medium speed 2 minutes or until light and fluffy. Add maple syrup and egg; beat well. Stir in buttermilk and vanilla with spatula.

3. Add flour mixture; stir until just blended. Spread evenly in prepared pan. Bake 15 minutes or until toothpick inserted into center comes out clean. Cool completely on wire rack.

4. Place jam in small microwavable bowl. Microwave on HIGH 10 seconds or until slightly melted; stir. Spoon over cooled crust; spread evenly with pastry brush or back of spoon. Cut into 16 squares.

ONE-BITE PINEAPPLE CHEWIES

Makes about 2 dozen cookies

½ **cup whipping cream**

¼ **cup sugar**

⅛ **teaspoon salt**

1 **cup finely chopped dried pineapple**

½ **cup chopped slivered almonds**

¼ **cup mini semisweet chocolate chips**

¼ **cup all-purpose flour**

1. Preheat oven to 350°F. Line cookie sheets with parchment paper.

2. Whisk cream, sugar and salt in large bowl until sugar dissolves. Stir in pineapple, almonds and chocolate chips. Stir in flour until blended. Drop dough by rounded teaspoonfuls about 1 inch apart onto prepared cookie sheets.

3. Bake 13 to 15 minutes or until edges are golden brown. Cool on cookie sheets 2 minutes. Remove to wire racks; cool completely.

KEY LIME BARS

Makes 24 bars

1½ **cups finely crushed graham crackers (10 to 12 crackers)**

¼ **cup packed brown sugar**

2 **tablespoons all-purpose flour**

5 **tablespoons melted butter**

1 **package (8 ounces) cream cheese, softened**

1½ **cups granulated sugar**

2 **eggs**

¼ **cup fresh or bottled Key lime juice**

1 **tablespoon grated lime peel**

Lime slices (optional)

1. Preheat oven to 350°F. Spray 13×9-inch baking pan with nonstick cooking spray.

2. For crust, combine graham cracker crumbs, brown sugar and flour in large bowl. Add melted butter to cracker mixture in two parts; stir until mixture is thoroughly moist and crumbly. Press evenly into prepared pan. Bake 15 minutes.

3. Meanwhile, beat cream cheese and granulated sugar in large bowl with electric mixer at medium-low speed until smooth and creamy. Add eggs, one at a time, beating well after each addition. Add lime juice and lime peel; beat just until blended. Pour filling over warm crust.

4. Bake 15 to 20 minutes or until filling is set and begins to pull away from sides of pan. Cool on wire rack 2 hours. Cut into squares; garnish with lime slices.

APPLE SLAB PIE BARS

Makes 2 to 3 dozen bars

1 package (15 ounces) refrigerated pie crusts (2 crusts)

1 cup graham cracker crumbs

8 tart cooking apples, peeled and sliced ¼ inch thick (8 cups)

1 cup plus 2 tablespoons granulated sugar, divided

2½ teaspoons ground cinnamon, divided

¼ teaspoon ground nutmeg

1 egg white

1 cup powdered sugar

1 to 2 tablespoons milk

½ teaspoon vanilla

1. Preheat oven to 350°F. Roll out one pie crust to 15×10-inch rectangle on lightly floured surface. Place on bottom of ungreased 15×10-inch jelly-roll pan.

2. Sprinkle graham cracker crumbs over dough; layer apple slices over crumbs. Combine 1 cup granulated sugar, 1½ teaspoons cinnamon and nutmeg in small bowl; sprinkle over apples.

3. Roll out remaining pie crust to 15×10-inch rectangle; place over apple layer. Beat egg white in small bowl until foamy; brush over top crust. Combine remaining 2 tablespoons granulated sugar and remaining 1 teaspoon cinnamon in separate small bowl; sprinkle over crust.

4. Bake 45 minutes or until lightly browned. Cool completely in pan on wire rack.

5. Combine powdered sugar, 1 tablespoon milk and vanilla in small bowl; stir until smooth. Add additional milk, if necessary, to reach desired consistency. Drizzle over bars.

LEMON POPPY THUMBKINS

Makes 2 dozen cookies

⅔ cup (1⅓ sticks) unsalted butter, softened

½ cup sugar

2 tablespoons grated lemon peel

2 egg yolks

1 teaspoon vanilla

1½ cups all-purpose flour

1½ teaspoons poppy seeds

½ teaspoon salt

¼ cup prepared lemon curd

1. Beat butter, sugar and lemon peel in large bowl with electric mixer at medium speed 1 minute or just until combined. Reduce mixer speed to low; beat in egg yolks and vanilla. Add flour, poppy seeds and salt; beat until just combined. Cover with plastic wrap; refrigerate at least 1 hour or overnight.

2. Preheat oven to 325°F. Line cookie sheets with parchment paper.

3. Shape dough into 24 balls; place 1 inch apart on prepared cookie sheets. Make deep indentation with thumb in each cookie. Bake 22 to 24 minutes or until firm but not brown. Cool on cookie sheets 2 minutes. Remove to wire racks; cool completely.

4. When ready to serve, fill center of each cookie with about ½ teaspoon lemon curd. Cookies are best served the day they are filled. Store covered in refrigerator.

RASPBERRY BARS

Makes 12 to 16 bars

1¼ **cups all-purpose flour**

¾ **cup sugar, divided**

½ **teaspoon salt**

½ **cup (1 stick) unsalted butter, cut into ½-inch pieces**

1 **egg, beaten**

2 **egg whites**

¾ **cup chopped pecans**

¾ **cup seedless raspberry jam**

1. Preheat oven to 350°F. Spray 9-inch square baking pan with nonstick cooking spray.

2. Combine flour, ¼ cup sugar and salt in medium bowl. Add butter; rub into flour mixture with fingers until fine crumbs form. Add egg; mix with fork until dough holds together. Press into a ball. Firmly press dough evenly into prepared pan. Bake 20 to 25 minutes or until crust is pale golden in color.

3. Meanwhile, beat egg whites in medium bowl with electric mixer at high speed until soft peaks form; slowly pour in remaining ½ cup sugar with mixer running. Gently fold in pecans.

4. Spread jam evenly over warm crust. Spread egg white mixture over jelly. Bake 25 minutes more or until top is lightly browned. Cool in pan about 1 hour. Cut into bars.

APRICOT OATMEAL BARS

Makes 9 servings

1½ **cups old-fashioned oats**

1¼ **cups all-purpose flour**

½ **cup packed brown sugar**

½ **teaspoon ground ginger**

½ **teaspoon salt**

½ **teaspoon baking soda**

½ **teaspoon ground cinnamon**

¾ **cup (1½ sticks) unsalted butter, melted**

1¼ **cups apricot preserves**

1. Preheat oven to 350°F. Line 8-inch square baking pan with foil.

2. Combine oats, flour, brown sugar, ginger, salt, baking soda and cinnamon in large bowl. Add butter; stir just until moistened and crumbly. Reserve 1½ cups oat mixture for topping. Press remaining oat mixture evenly onto bottom of prepared pan.

3. Spread preserves evenly over crust; sprinkle with reserved oat mixture.

4. Bake 30 minutes or until golden brown. Cool completely in pan on wire rack. Cut into bars.

SHAPED & ROLLED COOKIES

DANISH ORANGE COOKIES (ORANGESMEKAGER)

Makes about 2½ dozen bars

- ½ cup (1 stick) unsalted butter, softened
- ¼ cup sugar
- 1 egg
- ½ teaspoon orange extract
- 2 tablespoons grated orange peel
- 1½ cups all-purpose flour
- 4 ounces semisweet chocolate, chopped
- White sugar pearls or other decors

1. Beat butter and sugar in large bowl with electric mixer at medium speed 3 to 4 minutes or until light and fluffy. Beat in egg, orange extract and grated peel until well blended. Gradually beat in flour at low speed until well blended. Shape dough into a disc; wrap in plastic wrap. Refrigerate 1 hour or until firm.

2. Preheat oven to 375°F. Line cookie sheets with parchment paper.

3. Roll out dough on lightly floured surface to ¼-inch thickness. Cut dough into 2×1-inch bars. Place bars 2 inches apart on prepared cookie sheets. Gather and reroll scraps; cut additional cookies.

4. Bake 10 minutes or until lightly browned. Remove cookies to wire racks; cool completely.

5. Melt chocolate in microwavable bowl on MEDIUM (50%) 1½ to 2 minutes, stirring occasionally. Dip half of each cookie into chocolate, scraping excess on bottoms back into bowl. Place cookies on waxed paper; sprinkle with sugar pearls. Let stand at room temperature 1 hour or until set. Store tightly covered between sheets of waxed paper at room temperature.

ORANGE-ALMOND SABLES

Makes about 2 dozen cookies

¾ **cup whole blanched almonds, toasted***

1¾ **cups all-purpose flour**

¼ **teaspoon salt**

1½ **cups powdered sugar**

1 **cup (2 sticks) unsalted butter, softened**

1 **tablespoon finely grated orange peel**

1 **tablespoon almond-flavored liqueur *or* 1 teaspoon almond extract**

1 **egg, beaten**

*To toast almonds, spread in single layer on baking sheet. Bake in preheated 350°F oven 8 to 10 minutes or until golden brown, stirring frequently.

1. Preheat oven to 375°F. Reserve 24 whole almonds. Place remaining almonds in food processor; pulse until almonds are ground, but not pasty. Combine ground almonds, flour and salt in medium bowl.

2. Beat powdered sugar and butter in large bowl with electric mixer at medium speed until light and fluffy. Beat in orange peel and liqueur. Gradually beat in flour mixture at low speed just until blended.

3. Roll dough on lightly floured surface with lightly floured rolling pin to ¼-inch thickness. Cut dough with floured 2½-inch fluted or round cookie cutter. Place cutouts 2 inches apart on ungreased cookie sheets.

4. Lightly brush tops of cutouts with beaten egg. Press one reserved whole almond in center of each cutout. Brush almond lightly with beaten egg.

5. Bake 10 to 12 minutes or until light golden brown. Cool on cookie sheets 1 minute. Remove to wire racks; cool completely.

⇒ BLACK AND WHITE CUTOUTS ⇐

Makes 3 to 4 dozen cookies

2¾ cups plus 2 tablespoons all-purpose flour, divided

1 teaspoon baking soda

¾ teaspoon salt

1 cup (2 sticks) unsalted butter, softened

¾ cup granulated sugar

¾ cup packed brown sugar

2 eggs

1 teaspoon vanilla

¼ cup unsweetened cocoa powder

4 ounces white chocolate, melted

4 ounces semisweet chocolate, melted

1. Whisk 2¾ cups flour, baking soda and salt in medium bowl. Beat butter and sugars in large bowl with electric mixer at medium speed 3 to 4 minutes or until light and fluffy. Beat in eggs, one at a time; add vanilla. Remove half of dough to medium bowl.

2. Beat cocoa into remaining dough until well blended. Stir remaining 2 tablespoons flour into reserved dough. Flatten each dough into a disc; wrap in plastic wrap and refrigerate 1½ hours or until firm. (Dough may be refrigerated up to 3 days.)

3. Preheat oven to 375°F. Working with one type of dough at a time, place dough on lightly floured surface. Roll out to ¼-inch thickness. Cut into desired shapes with cookie cutters. Place cutouts 1 inch apart on ungreased cookie sheets. Bake 9 to 11 minutes or until set. Let cookies stand on cookie sheets 2 minutes. Remove to wire racks; cool completely.

4. Drizzle melted white chocolate onto chocolate cookies with fork. Drizzle melted semisweet chocolate onto plain cookies. Let stand about 30 minutes or until chocolate is set.

CHOCOLATE CHIP SHORTBREAD
⇒ WITH EARL GREY GLAZE ⇐

Makes about 3 dozen cookies

1 cup (2 sticks) plus
   1 tablespoon unsalted
   butter, softened, divided

½ cup sugar

1 teaspoon grated orange
   peel

2 cups all-purpose flour

¼ cup cornstarch

¼ teaspoon salt

½ cup mini chocolate chips

¼ cup boiling water

3 bags Earl Grey Tea

1 cup powdered sugar

1. Preheat oven to 300°F.

2. Beat 1 cup butter, sugar and orange peel in large bowl with electric mixer at low speed until combined. Gradually beat in flour, cornstarch and salt. Stir in chocolate chips; mix at low speed about 30 seconds until combined.

3. Roll out dough into ¼-inch-thick rectangle on lightly floured board. Cut dough lengthwise into 4 rows and diagonally into 8 rows. Place shortbread 1 inch apart on ungreased cookie sheet.

4. Bake 25 to 30 minutes or until bottoms begin to brown. Cool on cookie sheet 5 minutes. Remove to wire racks; cool completely.

5. For glaze, pour boiling water over tea bags in small bowl; let steep 3 to 5 minutes. Remove tea bags.

6. Mix powdered sugar and remaining 1 tablespoon butter in small bowl. Gradually stir in enough tea to make glaze thin enough to drizzle. Drizzle over shortbread. Let stand until set.

OAT, CHOCOLATE AND HAZELNUT BISCOTTI

Makes about 4 dozen biscotti

1½ cups whole wheat flour

1 cup all-purpose flour

1 cup old-fashioned oats

2 teaspoons baking powder

½ teaspoon salt

½ teaspoon ground cinnamon

1½ cups sugar

½ cup (1 stick) unsalted butter, softened

3 eggs

1 teaspoon vanilla

2 cups toasted* hazelnuts

¾ cup semisweet chocolate chunks

To toast hazelnuts, preheat oven to 325°F. Spread hazelnuts on baking sheet; bake 5 to 7 minutes. Place nuts in clean kitchen towel and rub to remove skins.

1. Preheat oven to 325°F. Line cookie sheet with parchment paper. Combine flours, oats, baking powder, salt and cinnamon in large bowl.

2. Beat sugar and butter in large bowl with electric mixer at high speed until light and fluffy. Beat in eggs and vanilla. Gradually beat in flour mixture at low speed. Stir in hazelnuts and chocolate.

3. Divide dough in half. Shape into logs 10 to 12 inches long; flatten slightly to 3-inch width. Place on prepared cookie sheet.

4. Bake 30 minutes. Cool completely on cookie sheet. *Reduce oven temperature to 300°F.*

5. Transfer logs to cutting board; cut diagonally into ½-inch slices with serrated knife. Arrange slices, cut-side up, on cookie sheet. Bake 10 to 15 minutes or until golden brown. Turn slices; bake 5 to 10 minutes or until golden brown. Remove to wire racks; cool completely.

LEMON CREAM CHEESE COOKIES

Makes about 3 dozen cookies

1¾ cups all-purpose flour

½ teaspoon baking soda

½ teaspoon salt

1 cup sugar

½ cup (1 stick) unsalted butter, softened

3 ounces cream cheese, softened

1 egg

Peel and juice of 1 lemon

½ cup shredded coconut, toasted*

To toast coconut, spread evenly on ungreased cookie sheet. Toast in preheated 350°F oven 5 to 7 minutes, stirring occasionally until light golden brown.

1. Preheat oven to 350°F. Whisk flour, baking soda and salt in medium bowl.

2. Beat sugar, butter, cream cheese and egg in large bowl with electric mixer at medium speed 3 to 4 minutes or until light and fluffy. Add lemon peel and juice; beat until well blended. Gradually beat in flour mixture and coconut at low speed just until blended. Drop dough by rounded teaspoonfuls about 2 inches apart onto ungreased cookie sheets.

3. Bake 10 minutes or until set. Cool on cookie sheets 4 minutes. Remove to wire racks; cool completely.

RUGELACH

Makes 3 dozen cookies

1½ cups all-purpose flour

¼ teaspoon salt

¼ teaspoon baking soda

½ cup (1 stick) unsalted butter, softened

4 ounces cream cheese, softened

⅓ cup plus ¼ cup granulated sugar, divided

1 teaspoon grated lemon peel, divided

1 cup ground toasted walnuts*

1 teaspoon ground cinnamon

2 tablespoons honey

1 tablespoon lemon juice

Powdered sugar

To toast walnuts, spread in single layer on ungreased baking sheet. Bake in preheated 350°F oven 8 to 10 minutes or until golden brown, stirring frequently. Cool completely. Place walnuts in food processor; pulse until ground but not pasty.

1. Whisk flour, salt and baking soda in medium bowl. Beat butter, cream cheese, ⅓ cup granulated sugar and ½ teaspoon lemon peel in large bowl with electric mixer at medium speed 3 to 4 minutes or until light and fluffy. Gradually beat in flour mixture at low speed until well blended.

2. Shape dough into three 5-inch discs; wrap in plastic wrap. Refrigerate about 2 hours or until firm.

3. Preheat oven to 375°F. Line cookie sheets with parchment paper.

4. Combine ground walnuts, remaining ¼ cup granulated sugar and cinnamon in medium bowl. Combine honey, remaining ½ teaspoon lemon peel and lemon juice in small bowl.

5. Working with one piece of dough at a time, roll out on lightly floured surface with floured rolling pin into 10-inch circle.

6. Brush one third of honey mixture over dough. Sprinkle with ⅓ cup nut mixture; lightly press nut mixture into dough.

7. Cut circle into 12 triangles with pizza cutter or sharp knife. Beginning with wide end of triangle, tightly roll up. Place cookies 1 inch apart on prepared cookie sheets. Repeat with remaining dough and filling.

8. Bake 10 to 12 minutes or until lightly golden brown. Cool on cookie sheets 1 minute. Remove to wire racks; cool completely. Sprinkle with powdered sugar.

HONEY GINGERSNAPS

Makes about 3 dozen cookies

2 cups all-purpose flour

1 tablespoon ground ginger

2 teaspoons baking soda

¼ teaspoon salt

⅛ teaspoon ground cloves

½ cup (1 stick) unsalted butter, softened

1½ cups sugar, divided

¼ cup honey

1 egg

1 teaspoon vanilla

1. Preheat oven to 350°F. Grease cookie sheets or line with parchment paper. Combine flour, ginger, baking soda, salt and cloves in medium bowl.

2. Beat butter in large bowl with electric mixer at medium speed until smooth. Gradually beat in 1 cup sugar until blended; increase speed to high and beat until light and fluffy. Beat in honey, egg and vanilla until fluffy. Gradually stir in flour mixture until blended.

3. Shape dough into 1-inch balls. Place remaining ½ cup sugar in shallow bowl; roll balls in sugar to coat. Place 2 inches apart on prepared cookie sheets.

4. Bake 10 minutes or until golden brown. Cool on cookie sheets 5 minutes. Remove to wire racks; cool completely.

ROSEMARY HONEY SHORTBREAD

Makes 2 dozen cookies

2 cups all-purpose flour

1 tablespoon fresh rosemary leaves,* minced

½ teaspoon salt

½ teaspoon baking powder

¾ cup (1½ sticks) unsalted butter, softened

½ cup powdered sugar

2 tablespoons honey

For best flavor, use only fresh rosemary or substitute fresh or dried lavender buds.

1. Whisk flour, rosemary, salt and baking powder in medium bowl.

2. Beat butter, powdered sugar and honey in large bowl with electric mixer at medium speed until creamy. Beat in flour mixture just until blended. (Mixture will be crumbly.)

3. Shape dough into a log. Wrap in plastic wrap; refrigerate 1 hour or until firm. (Dough can be refrigerated several days before baking.)

4. Preheat oven to 350°F. Line cookie sheets with parchment paper. Cut log into ½-inch slices. Place 2 inches apart on prepared cookie sheets.

5. Bake 13 minutes or until set. Cool on cookie sheets 1 minute. Remove to wire racks; cool completely.

⇒ CAPPUCCINO COOKIES ⇐

Makes about 5 dozen cookies

4 cups all-purpose flour

1 teaspoon baking powder

½ teaspoon ground nutmeg

¼ teaspoon salt

2 tablespoons milk

2 tablespoons instant coffee granules

1 cup (2 sticks) unsalted butter, softened

2 cups packed brown sugar

2 eggs

1 teaspoon rum extract

½ teaspoon vanilla

Semisweet chocolate, melted

1. Whisk flour, baking powder, nutmeg and salt in medium bowl. Heat milk in small saucepan over low heat; add coffee granules, stirring to dissolve.

2. Beat butter in large bowl with electric mixer at medium speed until smooth. Add brown sugar; beat until well blended. Add milk mixture, eggs, rum extract and vanilla; beat at medium speed until well blended. Gradually beat in flour mixture at low speed just until blended.

3. Shape dough into 2 logs, about 2 inches in diameter and 8 inches long. (Dough will be soft; sprinkle lightly with flour if too sticky to handle.)

4. Preheat oven to 350°F. Grease cookie sheets. Cut logs into ¼-inch-thick slices; place 1 inch apart on cookie sheets. (Keep dough chilled until ready to bake.)

5. Bake 10 to 12 minutes or until edges are lightly browned. Remove to wire racks; cool completely.

6. Dip each cookie into melted chocolate, coating 1 inch up sides; place on wire racks or waxed paper. Let stand until chocolate is set. Store in airtight container.

INDEX

METRIC CONVERSION CHART

VOLUME MEASUREMENTS (dry)

⅛ teaspoon = 0.5 mL
¼ teaspoon = 1 mL
½ teaspoon = 2 mL
¾ teaspoon = 4 mL
1 teaspoon = 5 mL
1 tablespoon = 15 mL
2 tablespoons = 30 mL
¼ cup = 60 mL
⅓ cup = 75 mL
½ cup = 125 mL
⅔ cup = 150 mL
¾ cup = 175 mL
1 cup = 250 mL
2 cups = 1 pint = 500 mL
3 cups = 750 mL
4 cups = 1 quart = 1 L

VOLUME MEASUREMENTS (fluid)

1 fluid ounce (2 tablespoons) = 30 mL
4 fluid ounces (½ cup) = 125 mL
8 fluid ounces (1 cup) = 250 mL
12 fluid ounces (1½ cups) = 375 mL
16 fluid ounces (2 cups) = 500 mL

WEIGHTS (mass)

½ ounce = 15 g
1 ounce = 30 g
3 ounces = 90 g
4 ounces = 120 g
8 ounces = 225 g
10 ounces = 285 g
12 ounces = 360 g
16 ounces = 1 pound = 450 g

DIMENSIONS

1/16 inch = 2 mm
⅛ inch = 3 mm
¼ inch = 6 mm
½ inch = 1.5 cm
¾ inch = 2 cm
1 inch = 2.5 cm

OVEN TEMPERATURES

250°F = 120°C
275°F = 140°C
300°F = 150°C
325°F = 160°C
350°F = 180°C
375°F = 190°C
400°F = 200°C
425°F = 220°C
450°F = 230°C

BAKING PAN SIZES

Utensil	Size in Inches/Quarts	Metric Volume	Size in Centimeters
Baking or Cake Pan (square or rectangular)	8×8×2	2 L	20×20×5
	9×9×2	2.5 L	23×23×5
	12×8×2	3 L	30×20×5
	13×9×2	3.5 L	33×23×5
Loaf Pan	8×4×3	1.5 L	20×10×7
	9×5×3	2 L	23×13×7
Round Layer Cake Pan	8×1½	1.2 L	20×4
	9×1½	1.5 L	23×4
Pie Plate	8×1¼	750 mL	20×3
	9×1¼	1 L	23×3
Baking Dish or Casserole	1 quart	1 L	—
	1½ quart	1.5 L	—
	2 quart	2 L	—